SCIENTIFIC BILLIARDS

by

WELKER COCHRAN
World's 18.2 Balkline Champion

Copyright © 2013 Read Books Ltd.
This book is copyright and may not be
reproduced or copied in any way without
the express permission of the publisher in writing

British Library Cataloguing-in-Publication Data
A catalogue record for this book is available from the
British Library

Billiards, Pool and Snooker

Cue sports, also known as billiard sports, are a wide variety of games of skill, generally played with a cue stick, used to strike billiard balls, moving them around a cloth-covered billiards table bounded by rubber cushions. Historically, the umbrella term was billiards. While that familiar name is still employed by some as a generic label for all such games, the word's usage has splintered into more exclusive competing meanings in various parts of the world. For example, in British and Australian English, 'billiards' usually refers exclusively to the game of English billiards, while in American and Canadian English, it is sometimes used to refer to a particular game or class of games, or to all cue games in general, depending upon dialect and context. The World Professional Billiards and Snooker Association (WPBSA) was established in 1968 to regulate the professional game, while the International Billiards and Snooker Federation (IBSF) regulates the amateur games.

There are three major subdivisions of games within cue sports: 'Carom billiards', referring to games played on tables without pockets, typically 10 feet in length, including balkline and straight rail, cushion caroms, three-cushion billiards, artistic billiards and four-ball. 'Pool', covering numerous pocket billiards games generally played on six-pocket tables of 7-, 8-, or 9-foot length, including among others eight-ball (the world's most widely played cue sport), nine-ball, ten-ball, straight pool, one-pocket and bank pool. And 'Snooker / English Billiards'; games played on a billiards table with six pockets called a snooker table (which has dimensions just under 12 ft by 6 ft). Such games are classified entirely separately from pool, based on a separate historical development, as well as a separate culture and terminology that characterize their play. More obscurely, there are games that make use of obstacles and targets, and table-top games played with disks instead of balls.

Billiards has a long and rich history stretching from its inception in the fifteenth century. Legendarily, Mary Queen of Scots was buried wrapped in her much loved billiard table cover in 1586. The sport has been mentioned many times in the works of Shakespeare, including the famous line 'let's to billiards' in *Antony and Cleopatra* (1606-7). There have also been many famous enthusiasts of the sport, including Mozart, Louis XIV of France, Marie Antoinette, Immanuel Kant, Napoleon, Abraham Lincoln and Mark Twain. All cue sports are generally regarded to have evolved into indoor games from outdoor stick-and-ball lawn games (retroactively termed ground billiards), and as such to be related to trucco, croquet and golf, and more distantly to the stickless bocce and balls. The word 'billiard' may have evolved from the French word *billart* or *billette*, meaning 'stick', and a recognizable form of billiards was played outdoors in the 1340s, reminiscent of croquet.

King Louis XI of France (1461–1483) had the first known indoor billiard table, and having further refined and popularised the game, it swiftly spread amongst the French nobility. Early billiard games involved various pieces of additional equipment, including the 'arch' (related to the croquet hoop), 'port' (a different hoop) and 'king' (a pin or skittle near the arch) in the 1770s. However other game variants, relying on the cushions (and eventually on pockets cut into them), were being formed that would go on to play fundamental roles in the development of modern billiards. The early croquet-like games eventually led to the development of the carom or carambole billiards category, what most non-Commonwealth and non-US speakers today mean by the word 'billiards'. These games, which once completely dominated the cue sports world have declined markedly over the last few generations. They were traditionally played with three or sometimes four balls, on a table without holes (and without obstructions or targets in most cases), in which the goal is generally to strike one object ball with a cue ball, then have the cue ball rebound off of one or more of the cushions and strike a second object ball.

Over time, a type of obstacle returned, originally as a hazard and later as a target, in the form of pockets, or holes partly cut into the table bed and partly into the cushions, leading to the rise of pocket billiards, including 'pool' games such as eight-ball, nine-ball and snooker. Today, there are many variations of 'billiards' including Straightline rail, Balkline and Three-chsion billiards.

Two-player or team-games such as 'Eight-ball', where the goal is to pocket all of one's designated group of balls (either stripes vs. solids, or reds vs. yellows, depending upon the equipment), and then pocket the 8 ball in a called pocket, or 'Nine-ball', where the goal is to pocket the 9 ball, through hitting (each time) the lowest-numbered object ball remaining on the table – have become very popular. 'Snooker' is largely played in the United Kingdom; by far the most common cue sport at competitive level, and a major national pastime. It is played in many other countries, although is unpopular in America, where eight-ball and nine-ball dominate, and Latin-America where carom games dominate. The first International Snooker Championship was held in 1927, and it has been held annually since then with few exceptions.

Welker Cochran, holder of the world's 18.2 balkline title.

To

Professor Lanson W. Perkins

who took me in hand at the age of fourteen and taught me the fundamentals of billiards, I dedicate this volume, with the fervent hope that it may be as helpful to my readers as his patient and kindly instructions were to me.

WELKER COCHRAN.

FOREWORD

Billiards is a game for all. Men, women, and children find in it a mild and beneficial exercise, a simple and wholesome relaxation, and a spirited form of competition that calls for a great deal of skill and ingenuity.

Few games offer all of these advantages—and the combination of them in billiards is the reason for its universal appeal. It is one of the world's oldest sports and its origin dates back to the dim days of antiquity. Reference to the game is made by writers as far back as 400 B. C.

Although the sport has developed and changed through the centuries, it has always been a favorite. Even as long ago as 1674, an author, describing various games, declared that billiards "for the excellency of the recreation, is much approved of and played by most nations of Europe, especially England, there being few towns of note therein which hath not a public billiard table, neither are they wanting in many noble and private families in the country."

To play some form of billiards is a simple matter. All that one needs do is to hit a ball around a billiard table, and sooner or later he will score a point according to whatever type of game it might be. But it is not human nature merely to want to play a game. All of us want to excel—and this book is designed to help make that desire a reality.

The author of it, Welker Cochran, for many years has been one of the outstanding figures in the billiard world. He has held championships at both balkline and three-cushion styles—an achievement as remarkable as though one were to set world's records in the 100-yard dash and the 2-mile run on the same afternoon.

Along with his wide knowledge of the game, Mr. Cochran also has a splendid insight into the problems of the average billiard player. He has written this book with the constant thought in mind that the greatest value of the printed word is to permit others to share the things that you have learned.

Using it properly, the beginner and the advanced billiard player alike will find this book a short cut to improvement and greater enjoyment—no matter what type of billiards they may play.

TABLE OF CONTENTS

Chapter   Page
Foreword   9

Part I—Billiard Fundamentals

1. Billiard Games   17
2. The Cue   23
3. The Stance   29
4. The Bridge   36
5. Making the Shot   40

Part II—Balkline Billards

1. English, Draw, and Follow.................   49
2. Massé Shots   57
3. Position Play   66
4. Rail Nurses   68

Part III—Three-Cushion Billiards

1. Balkline vs. Three-Cushion   75
2. The Three-Cushion Shot   80
3. Diamond System   85
4. Avoiding Kisses   88
5. Safety Play   90

Part IV—Hints and Suggestions

1. Art of Practicing.........................   99
2. In Conclusion 102
   Billiard Talk 106

TABLE OF ILLUSTRATIONS

	Page
Welker Cochran	Frontispiece
Balklines and anchors	18
Lagging, stringing, or banking	21
Balance of cue	24
Incorrect grips	26
Correct grip	26
Judging distance	28
Preparing to shoot: steps 1 and 2	30
Preparing to shoot: step 3	31
Improper positions	32
Correct bridge	37
Common, but poor, bridge	38
Bridge for rail shot	38
Bridge over object ball	38
Long bridge	39
Correct draw back	41
Follow-through	42
Draw, massé, and follow	52
Start of draw shot	53

Finish of draw shot	53
Start of follow shot	55
Finish of follow shot	55
Improper massé bridges	58
Correct massé bridge	59
Massé grips	60
Force massé grip	61
Making the massé shot	62
Rail nurse	69
Balkline nurse	70
Typical three-cushion shots	77
English	81
Center, draw, and follow shots	81
Running and reverse English	81
Effects of force	82
Diamond systems	86
Frozen cue ball safety	91
Bank shot safety	91
Safety vs. natural	92
Three-cushion shots	94-95

1. Billiard Games

BILLIARDS can be divided into two general classifications, the carom games and the pocket games.

In the carom games, the object is to strike the two balls other than the one with which the player is shooting. In the pocket games, the object is to drive the balls into receptacles or "pockets" with which the table is equipped. These pockets are covered by removable sections of the cushions for the carom games.

In all types of billiards, the player propels his ball with a tapered maple stick call a "cue." It is fitted at the small end with a leather tip, which is slightly roughened to impart various types of spin to the ball when it is hit.

The standard table is five feet wide and ten feet long. In the carom games, three balls $2\frac{5}{8}$ inches in diameter are used. In the pocket games, the balls are $2\frac{1}{4}$ inches in diameter and sixteen are usually used. For the latter type of billiards, the resilient cushions are eliminated in the corners and midway on each of the long sides of the table, where the pockets are to be found.

LITTLE TECHNICAL LIBRARY

Here, briefly, are descriptions of the different kinds of billiard games most popularly played:

Carom Games

Straight-Rail. The ideal game for beginners. The object is to hit both the other balls with your ball, known as the cue ball. This completes a point, or "carom." The cue ball may or need not hit the cushions (also referred to as the "rails") before and between its contact with the other balls.

Balkline. A device employed to prevent experts from gathering the balls into a corner of the table and making points indefinitely. Lines are drawn fourteen or eighteen inches from the cushions, forming eight spaces or "balks." When the two balls other than the cue ball (known technically as the object balls) come to rest within one of these spaces, the player is permitted either one or two shots before he must drive one of the object balls out of balk. It may return to

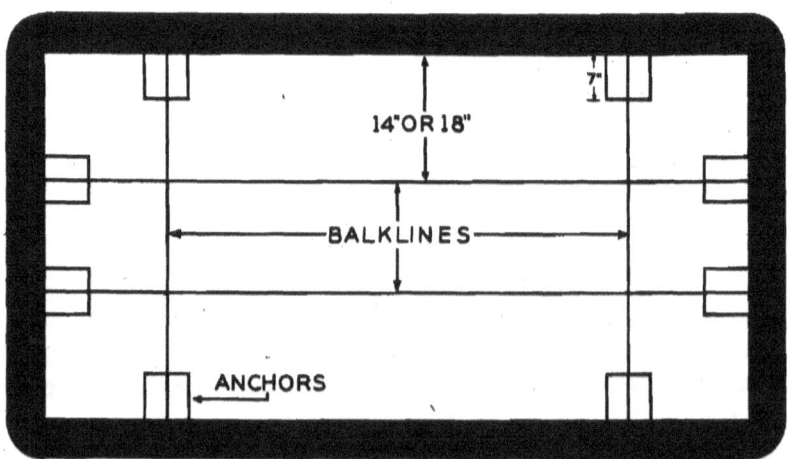

Diagram of billiard table top showing balklines and anchor boxes. Rules and methods of balkline games are treated fully in Part Two.

the same space, whereupon the player must again observe the same rule.

In addition to the balks, where each of the balklines intersects the cushion, an additional square seven inches high and seven inches wide is drawn on each side of it. When both object balls are in one of these rectangles, they are said to be "in anchor" and the balkline rules apply.

The three most popular types of balkline games are 14.2, 18.1, and 18.2. The first figure shows the distance from the cushion at which the balkline is drawn, and the second the number of shots permitted "in balk" or "in anchor."

Cushion Caroms. Similar to straight-rail, except that the cue ball must touch one or more cushions before completing the point.

Three-Cushion Caroms. The cue ball must touch the cushion or cushions three different times before completing the carom. All three impacts may be on the same cushion, but if the cue ball is in contact with a cushion ("frozen") before a shot, that cushion does not count as one of the three, even though the player may shoot directly at it. (Other special rules are covered in Part III.)

Pocket Games

Pocket billiard games are generally better known as pool games. The term pool came into usage a long time ago and has persisted in spite of a recent trend back to the original "billiards." It used to be the practice for each player to put a stake into a common "pool," the pool to be taken by the winner of the game; hence "pool."

There are a multitude of ways in which pool, or

LITTLE TECHNICAL LIBRARY

pocket billiards, is played, many varieties being confined to limited sections of the country. The rules for some of these games also vary in different localities. However, approximately 95 per cent of all competition is at the styles which are described here.

Rotation. This game is played with fifteen balls numbered from 1 to 15. The balls are placed on the spot in the form of an inverted triangle, with the No. 1 ball at the apex. The player opening the game shoots from the opposite end of the table with the cue ball, which thereafter is played from the position in which it stops. The object of the game is to pocket the balls in order, playing each time upon the remaining ball which has the smallest number. Any others which fall into pockets are credited to the player shooting, and at the end of the game the one with the largest number of balls to his credit is declared the winner.

15-Ball Pocket Billiards. Much like Rotation, except that the winner is determined by the total of numbers on the balls he has pocketed. The numbers total 120, hence the player who first makes 61 is the winner.

Pocket Billiards. (Also known as 14.1 Continuous.) The game is played with fifteen balls, either numbered or of solid red color. The game is started in a manner similar to other pocket billiard games, but on each shot the player must indicate the ball and pocket into which he intends to drive it. When fourteen balls have been pocketed, the balls are again "framed" with the apex of the triangle left vacant, and the game continues until one or the other player has scored the number of points agreed upon.

Starting a Game

All carom games open by determining the order

SCIENTIFIC BILLIARDS

in which the players will shoot. This is done by "lagging," which consists of driving a ball to the opposite end of the table and return. The one which stops closest to the rail from which the original shots were made has the choice of shooting or making his opponent take the lead.

When the order of play has been determined, the red ball is placed at the foot of the table on a spot halfway across a line drawn between the second diamonds on the long rails. This is usually marked on the table. The other white ball is placed on a corresponding spot at the head of the table (indicated by the plate showing the maker's name). The line across the table at the head end is called the "string."

The player who leads places his ball inside or below the string and within six inches to the right or left of the other white ball. On the opening shot he must hit the red ball first, but on all others (except when the balls are spotted again for any reason) he may play off either of the balls.

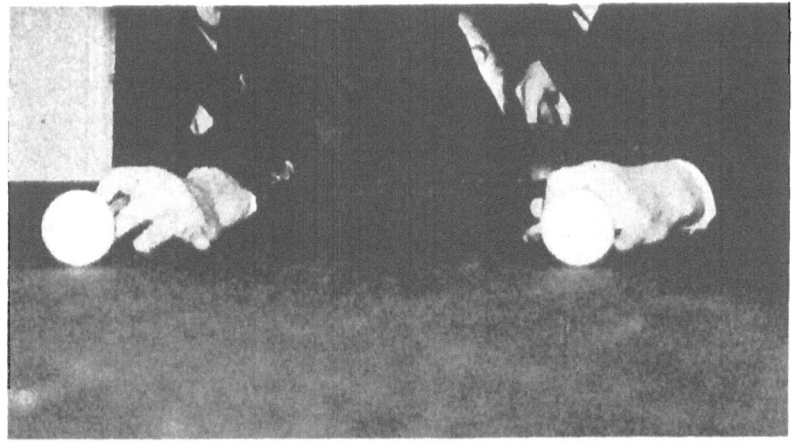

Lagging, stringing, or banking: The player whose ball returns and stops closest to the starting rail has the choice of shooting first or second.

LITTLE TECHNICAL LIBRARY

Pocket games are usually started by determining the lead either in the same manner as the carom games or by drawing numbered markers from a receptacle provided for this purpose. The opening shots have previously been described.

In all types of billiards, there are certain techniques which must be followed to obtain the best results.

A player must have a correct *stance* at the table. He must use a proper type of *bridge*. The *grip, force,* and *stroke* must be just right. He may have to put *English* on his cue ball to avoid a *kiss*. The shot may be a *follow, draw,* or *massé*.

All of these terms are explained fully under the proper headings, as well as in the introductory chapter. It is important that the reader have them firmly in his mind as he goes along.

2. The Cue

JUST as a hitter in baseball is lost without a bat to fit his particular physical requirements, so a billiard player is at a disadvantage unless he uses the proper type of cue.

Selecting a Cue

One of the questions most frequently asked of me is, "What kind of a cue shall I use?" In fact, any expert player probably hears this query more often than any other pertaining to the game.

The balkline player of championship caliber usually uses a cue that weighs 18 ounces and is about 55 inches long. (The weight of the cue is stamped on the butt in most cases. The cue of a three-cushion player is ordinarily from 21 to 22 ounces in weight and from 57 to 59 inches long.)

With balkline players in recent years switching over to the three-cushion game, one would think that they would change their cues. This, however, strangely enough, has not happened. Willie Hoppe and Jake

LITTLE TECHNICAL LIBRARY

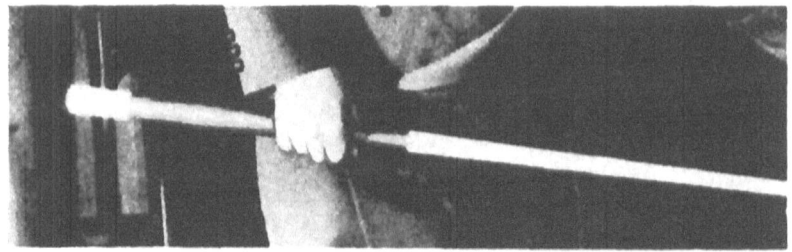

The proper place to grip the cue is about an inch back of the balance point, or about two inches behind the beginning of the twine wrapping.

Schaefer, among others, have continued to use their balkline cues with success. So have I, for that matter.

There is a reason for this. Most good balkline players have enough power in their stroke to make any three-cushion shot without adding weight or length to their cues.

For the average player, I should recommend a cue from 18 to 22 ounces in weight and 55 to 59 inches long. After once selecting a cue, continue to use it until you are thoroughly familiar with it. In time, you will get to know exactly what action you can get on the cue ball. Becoming accustomed to your cue is of far more importance than its weight and length. I am certain that neither Hoppe nor Schaefer would take my highly-prized cue as a gift if they had to use it in their match games—and neither would I accept theirs.

Briefly, the correct cue is the one to which you are accustomed. You need not be too finicky about selecting your cue. Pick the weight and length you like and then use it until you get "the feel." Once that is accomplished, your cue troubles are at an end.

The Tip

The most important thing about a cue, after all, is the tip. It is at this point that the cue comes into contact with the ball. If the tip is of poor quality or not properly finished, you will find yourself unable to get the best results.

Run-of-the-mill billiard-room players seem to prefer a rather soft tip, but this is not true of the experts. The latter invariably use a tip which is very firm. Usually their tips are pressed in a vise to make them even harder, although this can be overdone to such an extent that the tip will not hold the chalk.

The tip, in addition to being firm, should be rounded slightly. This allows the player to get more draw action and put more English on the ball than would be possible with a flat tip. All of the leading billiard establishments employ a cue man whose job is to see that all the cues are properly tipped, but in smaller communities where such men are not available, I have often seen cues with absolutely flat tips. The billiard players in such places face a hard task because overcoming such a fundamental handicap is rather difficult.

If your tip should get shiny and refuse to hold the chalk, take a piece of fine sandpaper, and without applying much pressure, roll the cue tip on it from left to right. The tip will quickly lose its gloss and will then hold chalk.

After a cue has been used, the tip should be gone over thoroughly before it is put away. A good tip is of the greatest importance to the greatest players, for without it they would be lost.

The Grip

Having chosen the proper cue and tip, you must next learn to hold your cue correctly. It is amazing how many billiard players err in this most fundamental step—one which is so vitally important.

LITTLE TECHNICAL LIBRARY

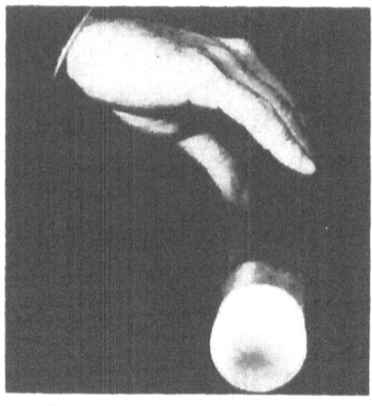 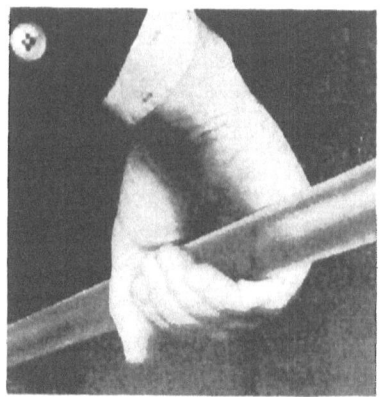

A fingertip grip is dainty but cannot guide the cue accurately.

A tight clutch locks the wrist and prevents free arm movement.

The most common fault is holding the cue too far back on the butt, which gives the cue a pump-handle motion while you are swinging it. This makes it impossible to aim accurately or to hit the ball effectively.

The proper place to grip the cue is usually about an inch back of the "balance." This is a point about two inches back of the front end of the twine wrapping of the butt. With a little experimentation you can easily determine the "balance" for yourself.

There are some exceptions. You can go back a little farther when you wish to hit the ball harder. Of course, there is a limit to how far back you can go. I

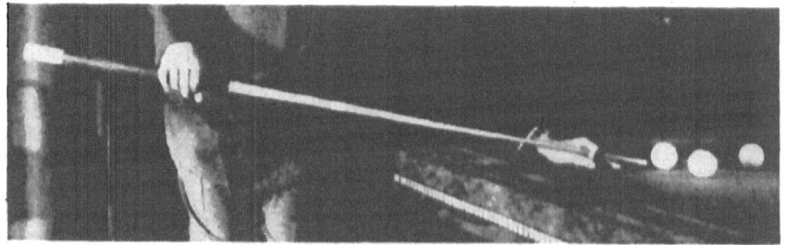

The proper way to hold the cue is with thumb and forefinger doing the main job, the other fingers supporting the cue firmly alongside.

should say that five or six inches back of balance should take care of any shot. Never hold the cue at its end unless you are reaching for a shot—and even then you would probably be better off if you used the bridge.

The proper point for holding the cue having been located, the next problem is the correct manner of gripping it. Hold the cue with the thumb and forefinger, with the other fingers alongside the cue, but not wrapped around beneath it. The cue should be held firmly with no space between it and the fingers.

Gripping a cue in this manner will give your wrist a chance to work in conjunction with the forearm. The wrist movement is what gives the player the effective blow that allows him to put excessive English on the ball, make long follow and draw shots, and otherwise play well. If you wrap your fingers around the cue, you will see at once that the wrist muscles tighten up and you will hit the ball with a stiff, ineffective arm movement. Too much emphasis cannot be placed on avoiding this fault.

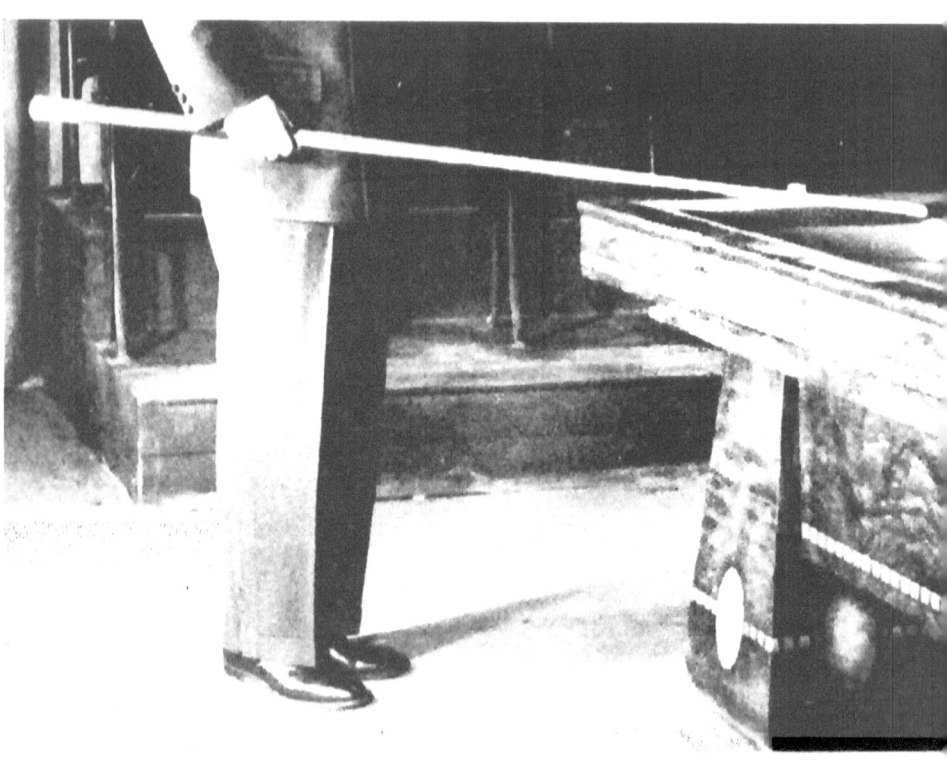

Holding the cue at balance, place your hand at your hip. If cue tip is just over the cue ball, you are at the right point for the shot.

3. The Stance

THE average billiard player never considers where he is placing his feet when getting set for a shot, yet if he is also a golfer, he is very careful indeed to have his feet just right before he swings.

There are hundreds of golf instructors who teach correct position daily to thousands of golfers, but in billiards I know of no one who had the patience and ability to teach these billiard fundamentals except Professor Perkins, my old teacher. He developed two professional world champions and one amateur titleholder, which should be proof enough that he had the right theory of how billiards should be taught. To Professor Perkins goes credit for all instructions on proper billiard form which are included in this book.

The first move in taking a proper stance is to place your feet together. You should be about two inches to the left of your line of aim. To determine the correct distance back from your cue ball, place your hand at your hip, and hold the cue at balance (see Page 26). When the tip is just over the top of the cue ball, you are at the right point.

Now take half a step forward with the left foot

LITTLE TECHNICAL LIBRARY

Having taken your stance with your feet together about two inches to the left of the line of aim, take a half step forward with the left foot along or parallel to the line.

Now turn slightly toward the right on the heel of your right foot, letting your weight rest on the right leg, as it should, and you will then be in proper position to shoot.

The forearm, from elbow down, should be nearly perpendicular to cue.

along the line of aim. Then turn slightly to the right on the heel of your right foot—and you have the correct position for your shot. Then settle back on the right leg, where most of the weight should be.

There should be a downward angle of about forty degrees to your upper arm from the shoulder to the elbow. If you have taken the proper stance, you will then find that the arm from the elbow down hangs in a perpendicular line.

In making your shot, the elbow is used as a pivot and should be stationary. The upper part of the arm does not move. The stroke is entirely from the elbow forward. This allows you to swing the cue in a straight and accurate manner. If you permit the upper part of your arm to move, too, you will develop

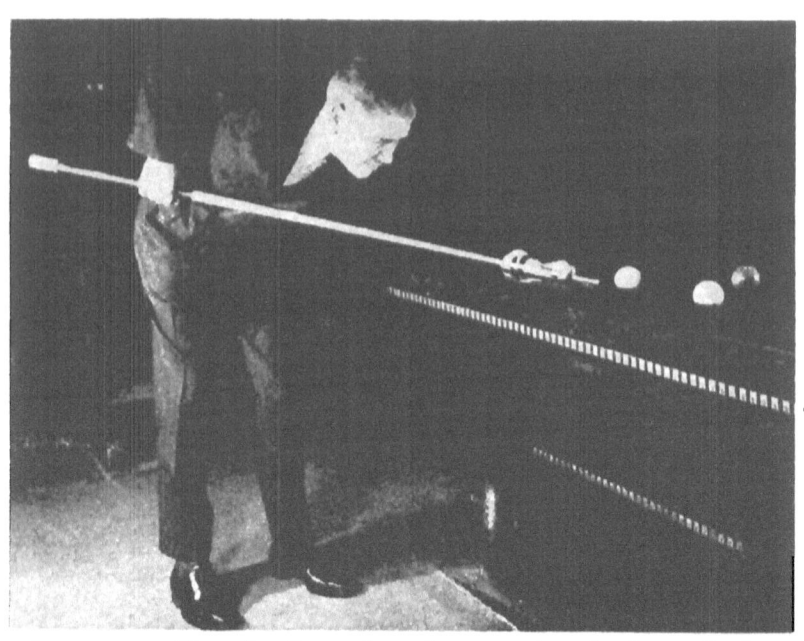
Improper position: Bending so low gives an awkward grip, spoils aim.

Starting too far back makes you lean forward and grip cue off balance.

the pump-handle stroke that will stop all chance of improvement in your game.

Here are some other common faults among billiard players and their causes:

Leaning forward. This is caused by being too far away from the shot. Anyone with this fault is handicapped considerably, as the body and aim are thrown completely out of line and it is almost impossible to deliver an effective and accurate stroke. If you have taken the proper stance, your head will be directly over your cue.

Bending too low. This is another common mistake, but one which can be easily corrected. If you keep your body more erect, you will find that, in addition to being far more comfortable, you have a much better view of the shot. Bending too low also causes the right arm to be raised too high, putting a muscular strain on the entire arm.

Turning to the right. This is caused by turning the entire body to the right, rather than the right foot. If you do this, you will find it difficult to get the proper perspective for the shot.

Perpendicular vs. Sidearm Stroke

Most expert players play with the right arm hanging in a perpendicular manner, and from a theoretical standpoint this is correct. However, several outstanding players, both past and present, have used what is known as the sidearm stroke. In using this stroke the arm is sometimes very nearly at a right angle to the body. Most players using this method have been more successful at balkline, where the balls are usually nearer the cue ball, thus eliminating the need for shooting great distances to the first object ball.

This method is usually acquired by those who learn billiards while they are too small to reach over the table, so that they have to hold the cue out to the side in order not to be bothered by the rail or cushion on the table. By the time the player grows taller and no longer needs to hold the cue in this way, the habit has become thoroughly set and the player assumes this to be the natural way to play.

When I went to Chicago to take lessons, I was a sidearm player and probably would have remained one to this day, had it not been for the instruction I received that cured me of this fault.

In my opinion, players who have succeeded when using a sidearm stroke have reached the heights in spite of this method rather than because of it. Any full-grown man starting out to copy this method would find himself up against a very difficult proposition, because it would be so unnatural. I mention this, because in my travels I have seen many players trying to develop a sidearm stroke—probably because they had seen a sidearm player on exhibition tours and, after watching him do miraculous things, had assumed that this must be the proper way.

Among three-cushion players, the sidearm stroke is rarely used. Willie Hoppe, outstanding billiard star of all time, used the sidearm while playing balkline, and later for three-cushion. In recent years, however, he has dropped his arm down considerably, doubtless because of the need for more accuracy on the long shots which are so frequent in the angle game.

Things to Remember

1. Be careful to place your feet so that you have a good balance and are in a comfortable position.

2. Keep your head directly over your cue and in line with your shot.

3. Be careful to keep your elbow stationary.

4. See that the stroke is from the elbow down, with the upper part of the arm not moving in the slightest degree.

5. Don't be careless in approaching the shot.

6. Don't take a grip too far back on the cue.

7. Use your thumb and forefinger to grip the cue. Avoid a "death grip" with your fingers tightly curled around the cue.

8. Don't turn your body to the right.

9. Make certain you are the correct distance back of the cue ball so that you will not have to lean forward.

10. Avoid a sidearm stroke.

4. The Bridge

ALL the description so far has been on how to hold the cue properly with the propelling arm. The other end of the cue is also vitally important; for no matter how perfect your form may be at the butt end, the execution of the shot is at the tip.

The front end of the cue is supported by placing the hand in a position known as the "bridge." There are many varied types of bridges—and most of those used by the average billiard player are incorrect.

The illustration (page 37) shows the most practical type of bridge for all billiard shots. The fingers are spread out as far as possible, making a larger and more solid base on which to rest the cue. The hand is turned slightly to the right by bending the wrist, and the forefinger closed entirely around the cue. The cue should run through smoothly, but no room should be left in this groove to permit the cue to wobble or get off line. You should also exert some pressure with the bridge hand, making it solid and immovable.

Bridges may be "long" or "short," depending on the force required for the shot. They are so called ac-

SCIENTIFIC BILLIARDS

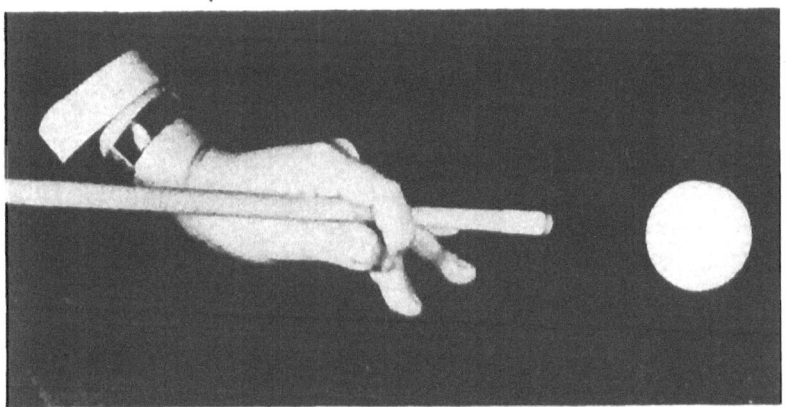

Proper bridge for most shots. Thumb and forefinger guide cue firmly.

cording to the distance the tip of the cue travels from the bridge hand to the cue ball. The shorter the bridge, the lighter the stroke.

A long bridge in billiards corresponds to the full stroke in golf and delivers the most power. When a golfer approaches the green and needs only a chip shot, he shortens his stroke to gain accuracy. The short bridge in billiards is similar in method and purpose.

Too many billiard players tend to use too long a bridge. Obviously, however, it is foolish to use a bridge a foot or more in length when a bridge of three or four inches would give you enough power to make the shot. Remember, the longer the bridge, the more chance there is for inaccuracy.

Once more I want to remind you that it is essential to hold the cue firmly in the bridge hand. Too many players fail to do this, and to overcome this one fault, grip the cue at the other end like a baseball bat in order to keep it going in a straight line. In other words, they are trying to overcome one mistake by making another. The right method is to employ a firm grip with the cue hand and a steady but relaxed grip with the other.

LITTLE TECHNICAL LIBRARY

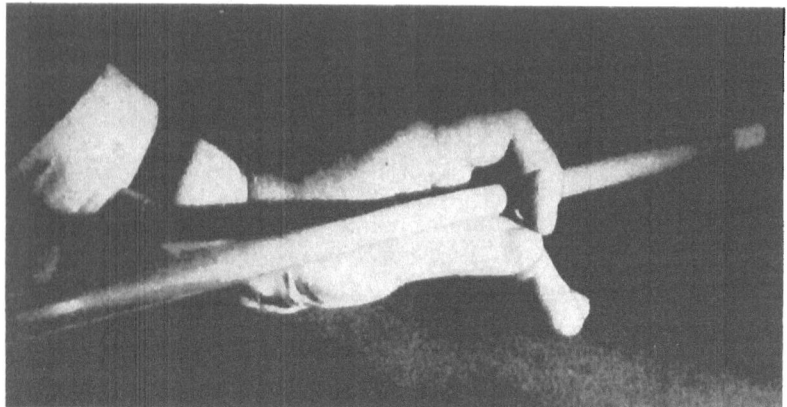

This commonly seen bridge is poor because cue cannot be firmly held.

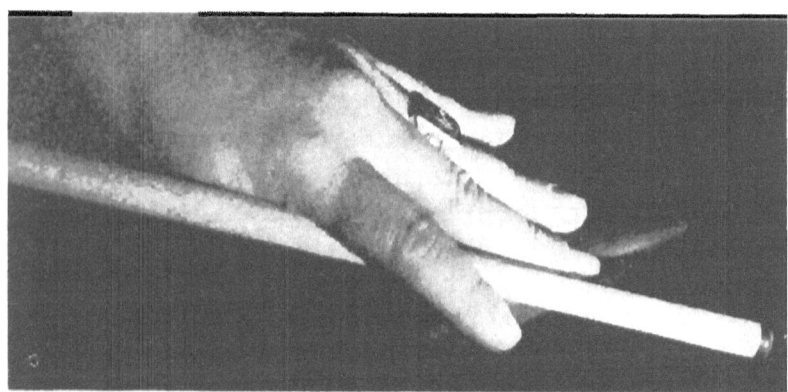

This is the correct bridge for shots that have to be made off the rail.

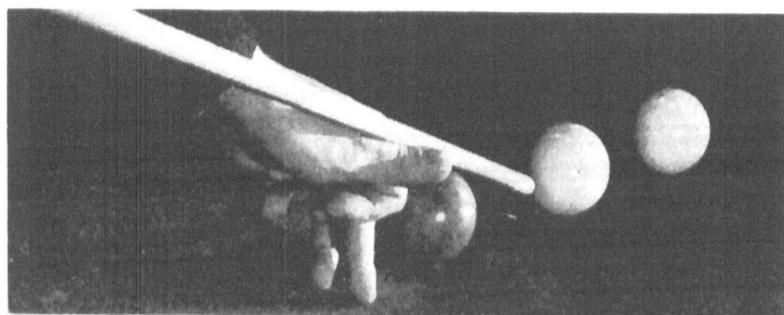

This is the bridge to use when the cue ball is between the object balls.

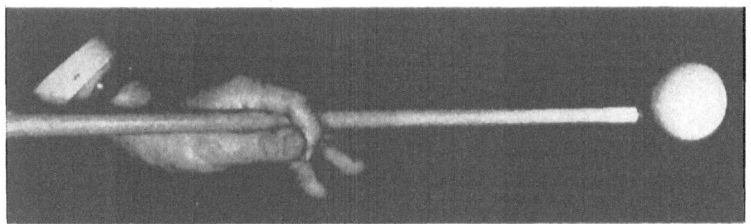

The longer the bridge, the more forceful but the less accurate the shot.

When the stroke is delivered, the bridge with the cue still in place should remain on the table in position until the ball is well on the way.

There are exceptions, of course, as when a ball is coming in your direction and you must get out of the way or foul the ball. But these exceptions occur only on rare occasions.

The average player is inclined to raise his bridge hand the moment he delivers the stroke—a constant invitation to inaccuracy. Keep your hand in position and be sure to finish your stroke before raising it. Your chances of success are much better if you deliver your cue through a fine, solid bridge hand. The "body English" you are anxious to use will not help the roll of the ball to the slightest degree.

Things to Remember

1. Hold the cue firmly in your bridge hand, with the forefinger wrapped tightly around the cue.
2. Do not raise your bridge hand until the ball is well on its way.
3. Don't use a long bridge when a short one will do.
4. Put some pressure on the bridge hand to make certain that it is immovable.
5. Make your bridge solid enough so that the cue cannot wobble or leave the line of the shot.

5. Making the Shot

WITH your feet and body in the right position, your bridge and grip correct, and a definite idea in mind as to how you are to make the shot, you are ready to take your stroke.

There is more to this than just stepping up and banging away. Certain precautions and preliminaries must be observed if you intend to improve your billiards. Some may seem trivial, but I can assure you that nothing is unimportant that helps the billiard player to acquire good form.

Preliminary to making the stroke, you should take four or five swings with the cue, just as a golfer "addresses" the ball on a tee. Do not waste any time aimlessly, but be sure to take enough preliminary strokes to get your shot properly lined up. I find that four or five are usually sufficient, although there are exceptions on unusually difficult shots.

On these preliminary strokes, the cue should be swung in a free, easy, rhythmic manner. It is important to avoid a choppy, jerky motion. The final draw back (the last before making the actual shot) is all-important. On it rests the success or failure of the shot.

The average player, in his anxiety to make the billiard, draws the cue back entirely too fast. The result is that he really hits backward and pushes forward with an ineffectual stroke. Care should be taken at all times to draw the cue back slowly. No matter how eager you are to hit the ball, don't fail to draw the cue back all the way for the final stroke, and at the same time don't hurry it. Like a duffer in golf, the average billiard player will speed up the draw back, which corresponds to the "backswing" in golf, if he wishes to hit the ball harder, and usually he gets inaccuracy rather than force.

The expert, when he finds it necessary to deliver an extra-hard stroke, will be unusually careful to see that his cue "gets around the corner" in a smooth, even manner. He saves the full force of the blow for the forward motion, rather than wasting it on drawing his cue back too fast. This doesn't mean that he won't vary the speed with which he swings the cue, for the harder the stroke, the faster the swing. But always you'll find that he has a smooth, rhythmic stroke—never a choppy, jerky one. It moves smoothly both ways.

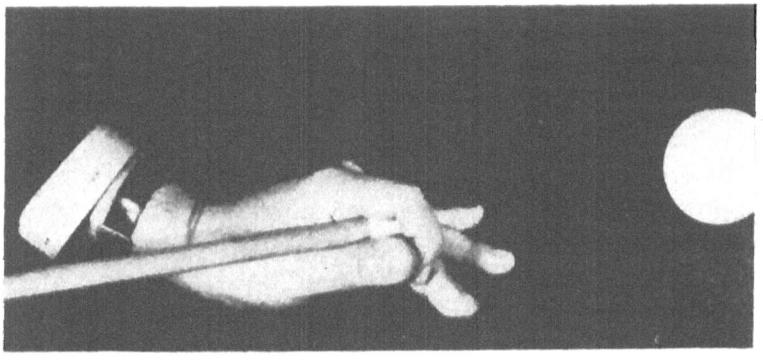

The cue must come all the way back—smoothly—before the final stroke.

LITTLE TECHNICAL LIBRARY

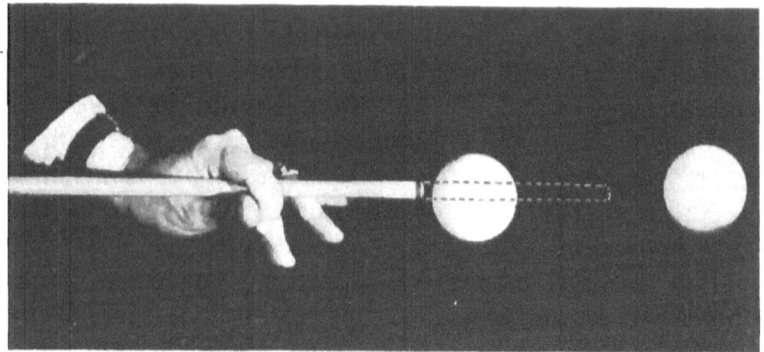

As in almost any other sport, the follow-through is all-important. It must continue unswervingly for several inches along the line of aim.

In billiards, as in any sport where a ball is hit with some sort of an implement, the "follow-through" is also important. Theoretically, the "hit" in a billiard shot takes place one or two inches before the tip of your cue reaches the cue ball. Then you should continue on your line of aim for from two to six inches more, depending on the power used in the shot. This is the follow-through.

The follow-through must continue along the line of aim—in other words, in a straight line. Here is one of the hardest things for an average player to learn. Invariably, his cue will veer to the right or left as he hits the cue ball, depending on where he wants the cue ball to go after striking the first object ball. Another common fault of this type of player is to raise or lower the cue tip while making the stroke.

The cue should go through the cue ball on exactly the same plane in which it started. Don't raise, lower, or move the cue to one side or another. No top-ranking player does. The fault is so universal among average billiardists that it is a good idea for you to check on yourself and see if you, too, are guilty of it.

Where to Look

Surprisingly enough, there is a good deal of controversy, even among expert players, on the subject of where to look in making a stroke. Some look at the first object ball just as they are about to make the final stroke. Others concentrate on the cue ball. My suggestion is to try both methods and use the one which gives you the best results.

Perhaps it might be better for the average player to look at the first object ball when he makes his stroke. I use the other method. I have always gone on the theory that if your stance is correct, if you have a grooved swing with the cue, if you have a solid bridge, and if you follow through correctly on your line of aim, there is only one thing left to do after you line up your shot—hit the cue ball in exactly the right spot. These are the reasons I look at the cue ball at the very last minute, but I can understand that this is difficult for the average player who has plenty of fundamental faults.

Therefore I repeat, try out both methods, and use the one which works best for you.

Where to Hit the Cue Ball

One question which expert players are frequently called upon to answer is, "Where shall I strike the cue ball on this or that shot?" There is no set answer. Each billiard shot is a problem unto itself. There are, however, a few general rules which may possibly help Mr. Average Player, in addition to the technical details on various types of shots described elsewhere.

In bank shots (shots in which a cushion is struck by the cue ball before it hits the first object ball), the cue ball should be struck opposite or slightly below center. Never hit it above center. A very slight amount of "running English" (English on the side in which you want the ball to go) is invariably used on bank shots. This is because a ball struck dead center does not take a natural angle around the table.

As a matter of fact, the great majority of shots in both balkline and three-cushion billiards are played by striking the cue ball either in the center or below it.

Calculating the Shot

Finally, I urge you always to make up your mind what you want to do before getting down to shoot. Most players have the fault of getting into position for the shot before deciding what they are going to do. Then they begin switching around, trying to determine the best thing to do. Obviously this handicaps the player.

Size up your shot carefully while you are in an erect position. Make up your mind just what you think is the best way to make it, and then, when you take your position, go through with it as you have planned.

Your judgment formed while you are erect generally will be far better than some idea you may get after you have taken the shooting position. If there is any doubt, step back from the table and start over. You will thus avoid many errors and misplays which come from changing your mind just before you shoot.

Speed of the Shot

Another thing to be considered in any billiard shot is the amount of force to be used. All calculations you make are based on hitting the ball at a certain speed. If you hit the ball harder or easier than you intended, you will find the result all wrong.

The more force you use, the more the cue ball will spread off the object ball; also the sharper angle it will take off the first cushion. In addition to these effects, the harder you shoot, the more draw or follow action will be produced.

Particularly in draw shots is the correct amount of force essential. It must be remembered that on a draw shot the cue ball does not go directly from one object ball to the other, but has a tendency to follow through a short distance before the draw takes effect. If the stroke is harder than planned, the cue ball is likely to settle too far through, and you will find that the draw action does not take place until too late.

Since all shots are played with different amounts of speed, you must know just how hard you intend to play before you can possibly make the correct calculations for the shot. Improper speed will cause you to miss just as many shots as faulty figuring.

Things to Remember

1. See that your cue follows through on your original line of aim.
2. Follow through on the same plane or level that you use in your preliminary strokes.
3. Hit the ball with a smooth, even stroke.
4. Concentrate thoroughly on each shot and make up your mind how you will play it before you assume shooting position.
5. Keep your eye on either the cue ball or the first object ball at the time you deliver the final stroke, depending on which system has proven to be most successful for you.

6. Don't allow your cue to veer to the left or right when you make your stroke. Keep the cue in the line of aim.

7. Don't use a sharp, jerky stroke to hit the ball. It will result in many miscues and will tend to render your stroke ineffective.

8. Don't fail to draw the cue tip back all the way to the bridge on your final stroke.

9. Don't hurry the cue on the final draw back. Take it easy and get the cue "around the corner" in easy fashion. Thus the chance for error is almost eliminated. It is on this phase of the game that most players, in their anxiety to hit the ball, go astray.

10. Don't fail to make up your mind completely exactly what you intend to do before you start the shot. Failure to decide results in many missed shots. If you want to change your mind, straighten up and back away from the table so that you can start all over.

11. Always consider the speed to be used before you make a shot. Use that speed, or your calculations will be way off.

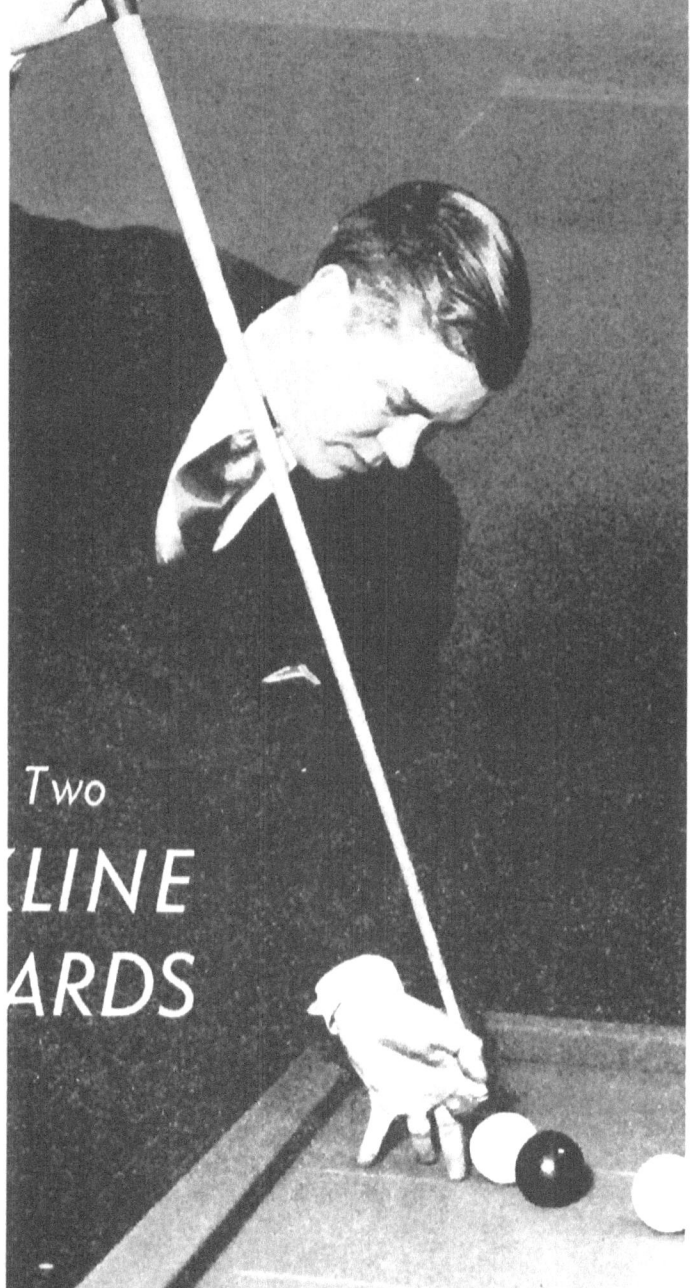

1. English, Draw, and Follow

MOST of the shots are the same in balkline and three-cushion billiards. Because proficiency in balkline is essential before three-cushion is attempted, this discussion will consider the shots from the standpoint of balkline. Later on, in the section on three-cushion, you will be shown how to adapt the shots to three-cushion play.

The first requirement in planning your shot is to determine on one which will give you the billiard. No matter how brilliantly you shoot, unless you score points it doesn't mean a thing.

The next matter to consider is that of bringing the object balls back into a position that promises a comparatively easy billiard.

Everything else being equal, always take the shot which will give you a point and at the same time gather the object balls into scoring position. If, however, the shot which will produce perfect position is one that is so difficult you may miss the billiard, forget the position. Make the point and the chances are that the next shot won't be any more difficult than the one you have just made. This seems to me to be the best policy.

In balkline, the theory is to drive the balls as little as possible. Take a short shot in preference to a long one. The farther you drive an object ball for position, the greater the chance for error. Whenever possible, drive the ball across the table, rather than up and down its full length.

Don't Drive Two Balls

Another important thing to keep in mind—and this rule has very few exceptions—is never to drive both object balls. You cannot do it with any consistent success. Drive one object ball and keep the cue ball close to the second object ball. Keeping close to them will give you much more accuracy and control.

Avoid massé shots (see page 57) wherever possible. Although the most spectacular of billiard shots, they are among the most risky. Even the expert players, all of whom are adept at making massés, avoid them whenever possible. If the cue ball rests in a slight indentation in the cloth, or on a tiny piece of chalk or similar obstacle, the shot is spoiled. As a result the experts avoid this type of shot wherever there is another method of making the billiard. That's a good rule for you to follow, too.

In balkline play, try to keep the balls near one end of the table as much as possible. Select the drive that will keep them in the end zone, rather than one which will gather them in the middle of the table. If the balls line up in a bad position while in the end zone, the player has several cushions and corners to aid him in making the shot. With the same position in mid-table, he has only the side rails to help him.

Avoid cushion play as much as possible. Most balkline shots are played from ball to ball. The one-cushion shot is used extensively in balkline billiards, but seldom the two-cushion or three-cushion shot.

Strive to master, by constant practice, the draw, spread draw, follow, massé, dead-ball, and one-cushion shots—and you can rate yourself as far above average. We shall now consider how to make these shots.

English and Its Uses

"English" is defined by Webster as "a spinning motion . . . given to a ball by striking it to the right or left of center." That's all there is to it, yet it remains a great mystery to a great many players.

The principles of English were discovered early in the nineteenth century by an Englishman named Jack Carr, who found that by hitting the ball in certain ways he could make it do queer things. The shrewd Mr. Carr didn't tell how he did it, but instead intimated that it was the result of the use of a special kind of chalk. He compiled a tidy fortune selling his chalk for ten shillings ($2.50) a box, and billiardists actually believed they couldn't get the effect without it. Finally a customer ran out of the magical chalk and used the ordinary kind—whereupon Mr. Carr's monopoly ended. The customer found the ordinary chalk worked just as well.

First of all, I want to caution you against using English unless you feel it is necessary to get the result you are seeking. Excessive use of English makes for inaccuracy. Many players, in their effort to put on a large amount of English, fail to deliver the cue straight through the cue ball. Their tendency is to let the cue tip veer to the right or to the left,

LITTLE TECHNICAL LIBRARY

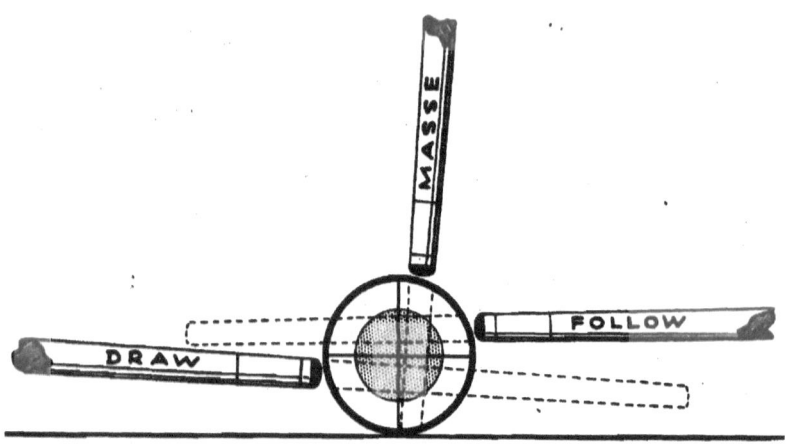

Correct points of contact between cue and ball for various shots. Cue must pass wholly through dark center area to avoid danger of miscue.

depending on the side on which they want to put the English.

It is essential, however, for a good player to be able to put maximum English on a ball in every style of billiard game. If he is unable to do this, a great number of shots become impossible.

Here are some important principles to remember about the use of English:

A cue ball struck above center tends to keep moving in the same straight line after contact with either a ball or a cushion.

A cue ball struck below center tends to swerve backward after contact with another ball or cushion. (See diagram, page 81.)

If a cue ball is struck by the cue tip to the right or left of its center, the ball will recoil from a cushion or an object ball to the right or left of its natural angle, depending on the side on which the English was placed.

English placed on the left side of the cue ball when it is aimed at the right side of the object ball (or vice

SCIENTIFIC BILLIARDS

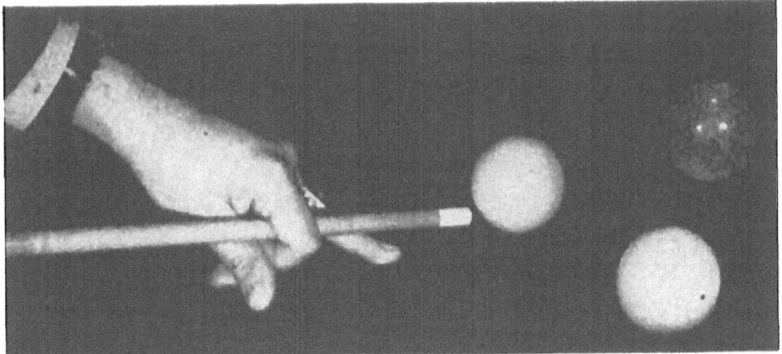

Start of a draw shot. Cue should have a slight downward angle. The further the cue ball is from the object ball, the lower it must be hit.

versa) is called reverse English and tends to reduce the speed and angle of the cue ball.

After contact with the cue ball, an object ball will proceed with English opposite to that which was given to the cue ball.

Draw Shots

The draw shot is one of the most useful in the repertoire of the billiard player. The ball is hit in such a manner that it tends to return in the direction of the force applied to it.

For a draw shot, the cue should have a slight downward angle. Then, if you follow through on this angle,

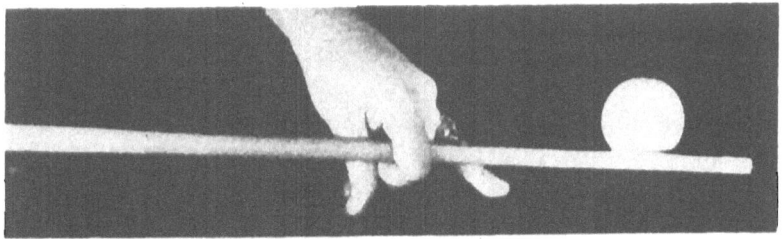

Finish of draw shot. Note slight angle between cue and table. Correct follow-through is vital. Tip of the cue should just touch the cloth.

you will find the cue resting on the cloth when the shot is completed. The further the cue ball is from the first object ball, the lower it must be hit to get the draw effect. The closer you are, the more effective is the draw, because then you don't have to hit too low.

The reason for this is that in a draw shot you must slide the cue ball until it comes in contact with the first object ball. Naturally, the further the cue ball is from the object ball, the more resistance of the cloth there is to overcome.

The follow-through, or finish, of the stroke is of the utmost importance in making a successful draw shot. A checked or jerky stroke almost invariably will cause a miscue. You cannot overcome this common fault merely by trying to make your arm go forward and thereby force the cue to follow through the cue ball. Following through is controlled by your mental condition; therefore you must train your mind.

After taking your proper aim, you should concentrate fully on driving the first object ball up the table or across the table, as the case may be. By all means, "think forward" but do not let your mind run to the second object ball. The only time the second object ball should come into your thoughts is at the time of lining up the shot and getting your aim. Forget it when you make your shot, and your miscues will disappear like magic.

Follow Shot

A draw and a follow shot are identical strokes, but not in the average player's mind. The strokes are identical, but players will invariably attempt to check their stroke on a draw and follow through on the follow. The result is that even the most inexpert play-

SCIENTIFIC BILLIARDS

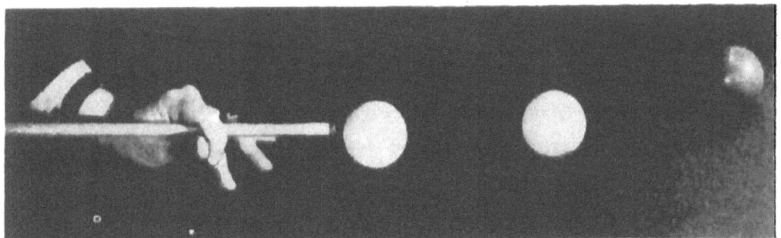

Start of follow shot. Cue is almost level. Avoid aiming too high. The further the object ball, the nearer center you must strike cue ball.

ers are fairly successful with their follow shots, while miscues are common on draw shots.

In a follow shot, the purpose is to make the cue ball continue in the same direction after hitting the object ball or cushion. The further the cue ball is from the first object ball, the closer to the center you must hit your cue ball. When you are near the first object ball, the higher you strike above center, the more action you will get on the cue ball.

Most players aim much higher than necessary. Striking too near the top of the cue ball may result in a miscue. On all follow shots, follow through smoothly with the cue for some inches (see illustration below).

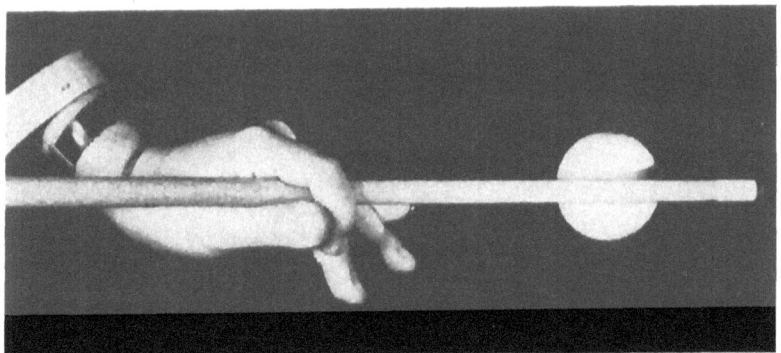

Good follow-through for a follow shot. Cue ball was replaced behind the cue in its original position to show the length of follow-through.

Things to Remember

1. Play for position, but don't sacrifice a point in the desire to bring the balls back to an advantageous spot for the next shot.
2. Don't use English unless necessary.
3. On a draw shot, follow through at the angle at which you shoot.
4. On a draw shot, the further away the object ball, the lower you must hit the cue ball.
5. On a draw shot, "think forward." Do not check the stroke to get the desired result. Hit the ball with a smooth, even stroke.
6. Don't aim too high on a follow shot or too low on a draw.

2. Massé Shots

THE massé shot is one of the more difficult shots in billiards, and is not very well understood by the average player. There are a few fundamental mistakes made by most players, and I shall try to make these clear.

First comes the question of the bridge to be used. Three of the fingers should be on the table, forming a tripod which will give your hand a solid foundation so it will not move while in the act of delivering the stroke. The wrist should be so turned that when the bridge is made, the palm of the hand will be toward the cue ball. The forefinger is raised out of the way by bending the middle joint. By turning the hand so that the palm faces the ball, you will find it is natural for the cue to stay in the bridge groove without your gripping it too tightly with the upper hand.

Most players put their bridge hand on the table with the back of the hand facing the cue ball, and when this is done, you will find you have only two fingers resting on the cloth, and the small one, which should be on the table, will be of no use to you. It

LITTLE TECHNICAL LIBRARY

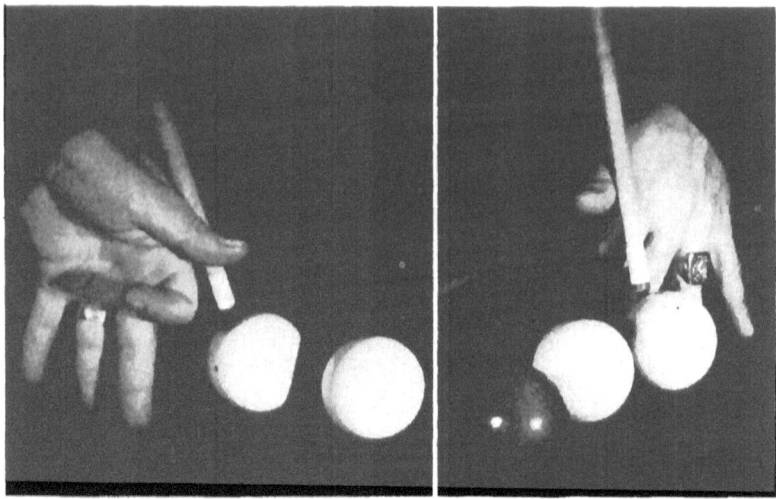

Improper massé bridges. It is impossible to get proper support for this difficult stroke with only two fingers resting insecurely on the table.

is impossible to get a solid bridge with only two fingers on the table.

In order to overcome this very common fault, turn your wrist as if to "palm" the ball, and you will find the little finger can then be made to rest on the cloth, forming the tripod which makes for solidity. Failing to "palm" the ball in this manner causes the cue to have a tendency to fly up or off the bridge hand, and as a result the player is inclined to grip the cue in a vise-like manner with the right hand to keep the cue in place. The moment you take a death grip with the right hand, you are no longer able to produce a massé action on the cue ball.

The massé stroke is made by using the wrist action just as in other shots, and, of course, the moment your muscles become tightened up trying to hold the cue on the bridge, wrist action is impossible. The first thing to practice and master is the bridge, and, after you have learned to turn your wrist and hand into the correct position, you will find it unnecessary to grip the cue so hard with the upper hand. Then you will be free to take a firm but relaxed grip with the upper hand, which in turn will allow you to use the wrist in delivering the most effective stroke.

There are three ways of gripping the cue with the right hand. The first, which I do not favor, consists in using only the forefinger and thumb. Preferred to this method is the second style, using the forefinger, thumb, and middle finger, which will give you much better control and power. This grip is useful when reaching out into the middle of the table for a difficult shot.

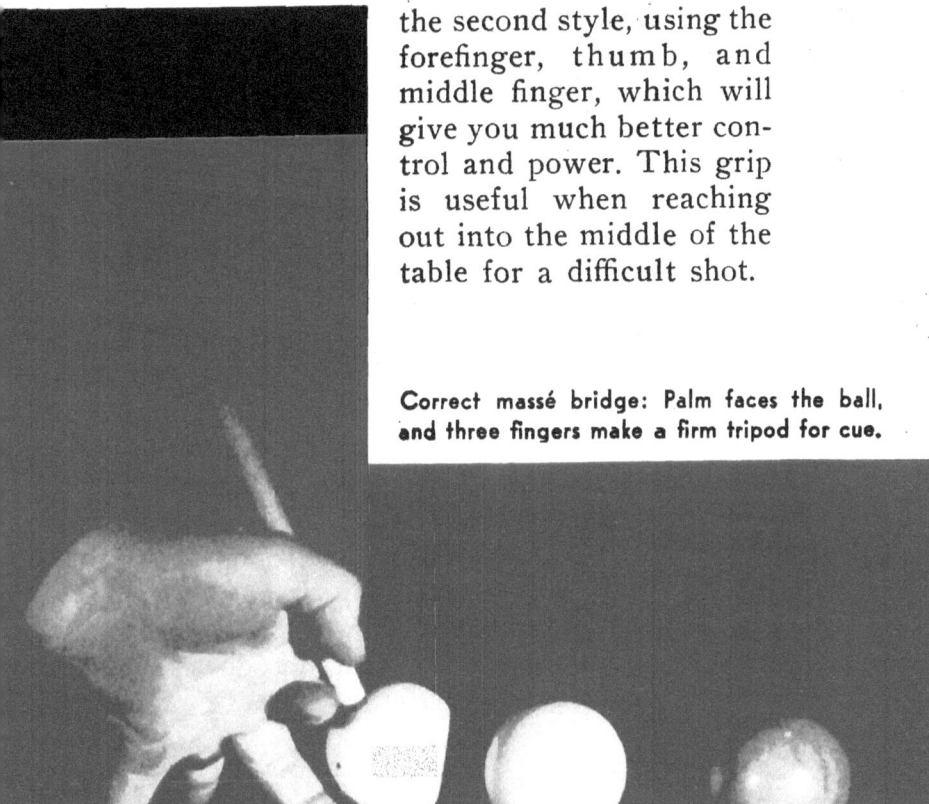

Correct massé bridge: Palm faces the ball, and three fingers make a firm tripod for cue.

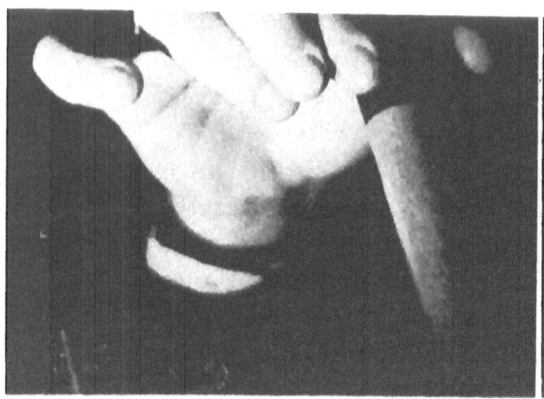 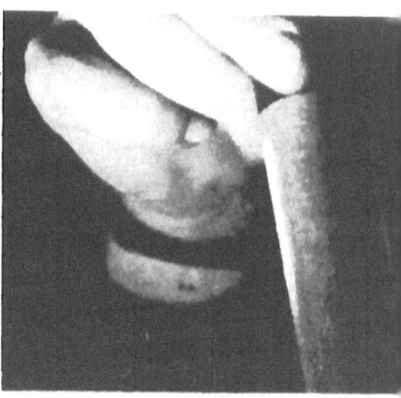

The thumb and forefinger grip for a massé shot leaves you without complete control.

This grip, using the middle finger well, gives better control and power

The third grip is similar to the grip used in your regular play, except that the hand is turned over as the cue is raised to an upright position. This grip is by far the most popular and with it you have much more power at your command.

The Stroke

The massé stroke is not a sharp peck at the ball, as many people seem to think. To see the average player make a massé stroke, you would think he was striking an egg shell and did not want to break it. The fact is, you must follow through just as in any other class of shot.

Striking the cloth with the cue tip on the follow through will not do any damage. Cloths are torn because the player has too much slant or angle to his cue—in other words, because he does not elevate his cue enough. This allows the edge of the tip to strike the cloth. In this way a thread may be cut. On most massé strokes the cue is held very nearly in a perpendicular line. But here is an important point that you must consider on each and every massé shot. The angle of the cue is governed by the amount of curve you wish the cue ball to take. The sharper and more pronounced the curve you wish to produce, the more elevation required. The less severe the curve and the more forward you wish the cue ball to travel, the less elevation necessary. It is when the cue has only a slight elevation that you must be careful of tearing the cloth with the tip.

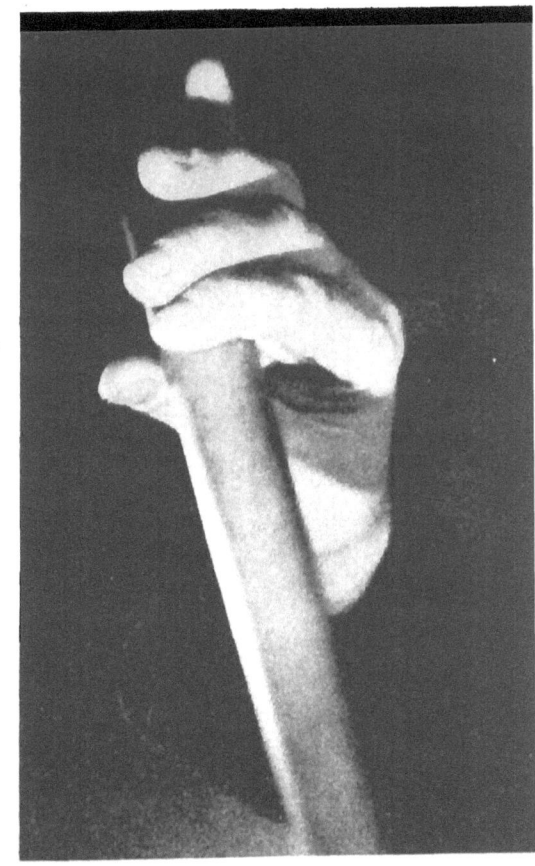

This grip resembles the one used in regular play except that the hand is turned over as the cue is raised for the massé stroke. It is the most popular grip for this stroke and gives greatest power.

Illustration A demonstrates grip and position for applying slight extra force. B shows a difficult grip when great extra power is needed; left elbow is held hard against the body to steady the bridge. C shows a most common massé grip, very useful when you have to reach for your shot.

The cue should be swung in the same smooth and even manner as in any other stroke. Get away from the idea that you are striking an egg shell and may break it. Let the cue follow through in a smooth, even fashion, just as on any other shot.

Assuming that you can now make the correct bridge, which in turn allows you to take a relaxed grip with the right hand, I shall next discuss where to hit the cue ball. In your mind's eye, draw a line through the center of your cue ball on your "line of aim." Now draw a line exactly at right angles across the ball, in this way cutting the ball into four parts. The proper place to hit the cue ball is in the center of the rear quarter, located on the side of the ball toward which the curve is to take place. In other words, if the curve is to be to the right, then hit in the center of the rear quarter on the right-hand side. Be sure the first imaginary line you draw is on your line of aim, for the proper quartering of the ball depends entirely upon your first imaginary line being correct.

Cue Points Through Ball

Your cue should be pointing through the ball to or near the point on the cloth on which the ball rests. This is important and failure to hit through to where the ball rests on the cloth causes most of the miscues which are so common on massé shots.

You can lengthen or shorten the curve the ball will take simply by raising or lowering the elevation of the cue. If you can learn to strike the cue ball in the proper place, don't spoil the shot by neglecting to have the cue tip point through to where the ball rests on the cloth. Pinching the ball into the cloth causes the ball to spin and curve. Hitting the cue ball in the right spot will not get results unless the cue is pointing in the right direction.

Remember, as you raise or lower the angle of your cue and change your line of aim, the center of the cue ball with reference to your cue continually changes. The general fault among players is to get too far on the edge of the ball, or too far in the rear. Either will cause you to slip off, or miscue, regardless of how well you may deliver the stroke. Get up more on the ball. If you can learn to draw the lines correctly in your mind's eye, you will find the spot to hit well up on the ball, and not on the edge or too far back.

Massé shots are usually eliminated by the better players when the cue ball is more than a foot from the first object ball. The further the player is from the first object ball, the less accuracy he can expect. Under these conditions he should try to find another type of shot.

The massé is one of the most useful shots in the game for the expert player. Because of the continual driving of the balls together for position, it is inevitable that the balls will line up a certain number of times. Without perfect control of the massé an expert would be utterly lost.

Bridge, Grip, Wrist

Concentrate first on making the solid tripod bridge with the palm of the hand toward the cue ball; then upon obtaining a relaxed grip on the cue with the right hand, using either of the two grips described. Be sure to get the wrist into the shot. Next select the spot on the cue ball to strike, and be sure your cue is pointing through to where the ball rests on the cloth. Take care to regulate the amount of elevation of the cue according to the amount of curve you wish to produce. Finally, follow through smoothly.

Things to Remember

1. Avoid massé shots unless it is impossible to make the point in any other manner.
2. Your bridge is the most important part of a massé shot. Be sure that it is correct.
3. On a massé shot, don't just peck at the ball. Follow through down to the cloth. If you are holding the cue correctly you won't injure the cloth.

3. Position Play

AIMLESS knocking of the balls around will not improve your average in balkline. You must make every shot with the thought in mind that when the balls come to rest, you will have "good position" for the next one.

What Is Good Position?

The shot should give you the choice of the most cushions, the balls should be close to the cushions, and the cue ball should be near the object balls. The theory of good billiards is to avoid the necessity of having to make hard shots. Trick shots and fancy shots are spectacular, but one can scarcely run up clusters of points with them.

Position play is an advanced phase of billiards on which some fine books have been written. It is too involved and too lengthy to be included here, but some important rules have been evolved which will be helpful to you in striving for position play, even though you do not delve deeper into the subject.

They are:
1. Drive as little as possible.
2. The shorter drive is usually the best.
3. Don't drive both balls.
4. Second object ball should not be driven.
5. Keep balls at end of table.
6. Keep cue ball close to object balls if possible.
7. Keep object balls faced toward end rails.
8. Don't get cue ball between object balls.
9. Keep cue ball away from the rails.
10. Keep cue ball a few inches away from object ball to avoid "line-ups."
11. Don't let your cue ball travel too fast.
12. If impossible to bring balls back into position, leave one object ball near a corner.

My recommendation is to study position play if you want to take your place among the experts.

Don't try to play balkline billiards (with the lines on the table) until you have learned the rudiments of straight-rail play, particularly the ability to nurse the balls along the table as outlined in succeeding pages. And, as I have said before, sacrifice position to make your point.

4. Rail Nurses

WHEREVER you go throughout the country, you will see balkline attempted daily by players who are far from ready for such a difficult game. Ordinary straight-rail billiards involves all the necessary strokes and technique required in the more difficult game of balkline. Any player who prefers balkline should continually practice ball-to-ball billiards until he is able to make runs of fifty or even one hundred with some degree of consistency.

My teacher never allowed me to play balkline until I had thoroughly mastered straight-rail. He gave me the task of learning to take the balls twice around the table without losing the "rail nurse." After many months and countless hours of hard work, the happy day finally arrived, and from then on I gave up straight-rail billiards and concentrated on balkline. However, to this day when I am practicing for tournament play, I always make it a rule to put in some time on the "rail nurse."

The theory of this "nurse" is to keep the outside object ball going in a straight line slightly ahead of

SCIENTIFIC BILLIARDS

the inside ball which goes into the cushion and out with almost every stroke. The moment the outside ball gets too far out from the rail or too far ahead of, or behind the first object ball, the rail nurse is lost, and it is time to replace the balls and start over.

It is a grand problem for one who likes to study the action of billiard balls, the effect of English on the object balls, and so forth. You will find this nurse a never-ending study.

The general public watches a great balkline expert manipulate the balls for long runs of two or three hundred, but seldom has any idea how it is done. Learning the rail nurse is where all of the great players have learned how to control the three balls. This also develops a delicate sense of touch, or "feel," so necessary in billiards. The balkline nurse that you no doubt have seen played and marveled at, is simply the rail nurse played from eighteen inches off the rail. Naturally, driving the balls eighteen inches to the rail and eighteen inches back makes it impossible to

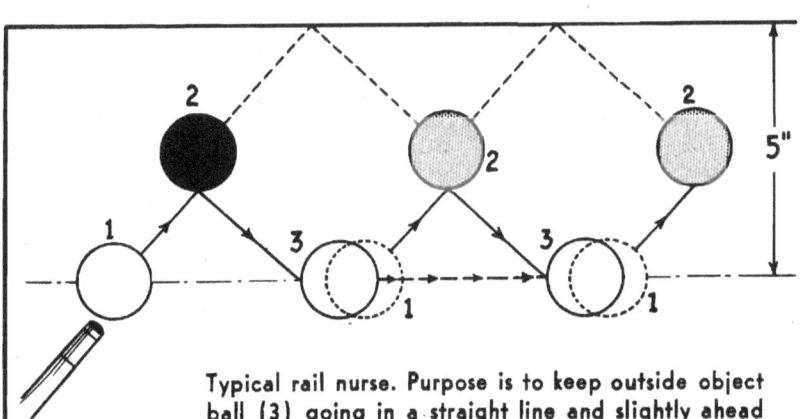

Typical rail nurse. Purpose is to keep outside object ball (3) going in a straight line and slightly ahead of the inside ball (2), which goes in to hit the cushion and rebound out with almost every stroke. If the outside ball gets too far out from the rail, or too far ahead of (2), the nurse is lost.

LITTLE TECHNICAL LIBRARY

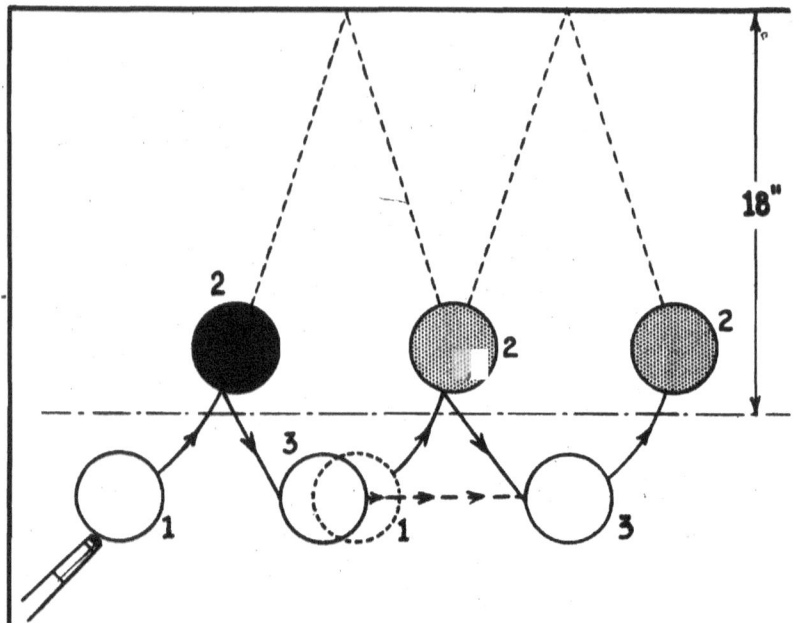

The balkline nurse: This is simply the rail nurse played from eighteen inches off the cushion. The longer drive makes accuracy more difficult.

run thousands of billiards without a miss, which can be accomplished by experts at the rail nurse. It goes back to the old theory: the further you drive the balls, the less accuracy is possible.

George Sutton, of Chicago, was one of the outstanding "balkline nurses," and later Eduard Horemans, of Belgium, was exceptional. Of course, leading players execute all of their nurses and strokes almost perfectly, otherwise they would have weaknesses which would prevent them from being the outstanding players of the day. However, certain players favor certain shots, or nurses. Sutton and Horemans continually tried to get the balls in position for the balkline nurse, and for their ability to play this nurse they were famous.

In the rail or balkline nurse you must keep the object balls in front of your cue ball. If your cue ball gets ahead of the first object ball, you will find the nurse is lost, as it is impossible to bring this ball up into the proper position again.

It will take great patience, perseverance, and thought to master the rail nurse, but if you are willing to make the effort, I am sure you will find the time spent of great benefit to your game. I know of no other single style of practice that will produce more beneficial results. Balkline is a game of manipulation of the balls and without a clear insight into the intricacies of the rail nurse, I fail to see how a player can ever hope to know exactly what to do with the balls at balkline.

My advice is to play straight-rail billiards until you are able to run fifty or more pretty consistently. Then put the balklines on the table and see if the game does not appear somewhat more simple to you. All of the greatest players have gone through the same practice, only to a far greater extent. Where I suggest that you learn to run fifty or one hundred, they have learned to run thousands.

The rail nurse is the very foundation of billiards as far as manipulation of the balls and position play are concerned. If this practice is so vital and necessary to the great experts, it surely will not do your game any harm. You will find it tedious and trying at times, but if you are anxious to improve your game, the time will be well spent.

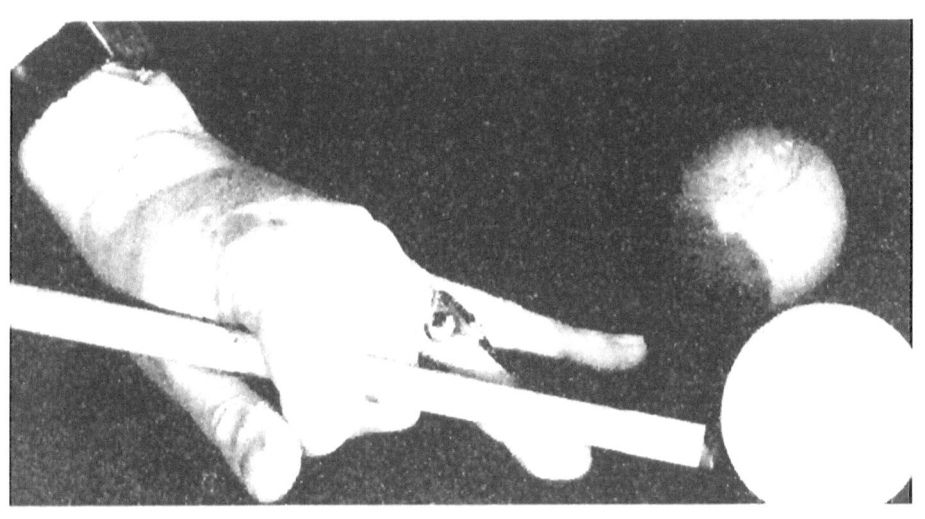

1. Balkline vs. Three-Cushion

THROUGHOUT the years I have had thousands of persons ask me which of the two games, balkline or three-cushion billiards, is the more difficult. The general opinion among the public is that three-cushion is harder to play. I assure you that this is not true. This misunderstanding probably arose because it is possible to make runs of several hundred points in balkline without missing, whereas in three-cushion seven or eight is considered a fine run. The world's record at 18.2 is 432, but at three-cushion it is only eighteen.

I feel qualified to discuss this controversial subject, as I believe I am the only player fortunate enough to have won and held both of these world titles at the same time. For this reason, no one can think that my opinion is prejudiced. If a balkline expert who was not adept at three-cushion discussed this subject, no doubt he would favor balkline, and the three-cushion player who can never be expert at balkline speaks loudly and clearly in favor of his particular game. Having attained top rank in both at the same time, I can see the good and bad points of each.

LITTLE TECHNICAL LIBRARY

In my opinion each game has its niche to fill. If you are one of those players who assume that three-cushion is more difficult because it is harder to make large runs, I must say emphatically that I think you are wrong. Balkline is an absolute science into which luck enters probably less than in any other game played. The player must have perfect control of all three balls on every shot he plays.

Speed is absolutely vital in balkline. Driving an object ball twenty feet or more and having it come back consistently within an inch or so of where you want it is not an easy task. It requires accuracy and precision not essential to three-cushion players.

Balkline requires far more delicacy of stroke and accuracy and also a so-called "touch," or feel of the shot which is not vital in three-cushion billiards. A balkline player must learn to concentrate deeply over long periods of time while he is compiling a large run. Failure for one moment to concentrate fully will lead to a poor shot which is likely to cause him to lose control of the balls and ultimately break the run.

In three-cushions this deep concentration is not vital, as it is a game composed more of individual shots, no one having particular bearing on another. True, there are shots which call for position play in the three-cushion game, but they are exceptions. In three-cushion the player plays to make the billiard and then tries to solve the next problem. If this procedure were used in balkline, a run of forty or fifty points would be a great feat.

The massé shot is essential in balkline to extricate yourself from difficult positions caused by the balls lining up, but in three-cushion this shot is practically never used. It takes years of hard work for a balkline player to become master of the massé. Without it the

SCIENTIFIC BILLIARDS

balkline player would be a complete failure, but in the other style of play the shot is unnecessary. "Nip" draws and close follows are regular shots used very often in balkline but only frequently in three-cushion.

In balkline play the player will use probably six or eight different forms of bridge, while half that number will suffice for three-cushion play. There are literally dozens of things to be mastered in balkline that never are used in three-cushion. These are the

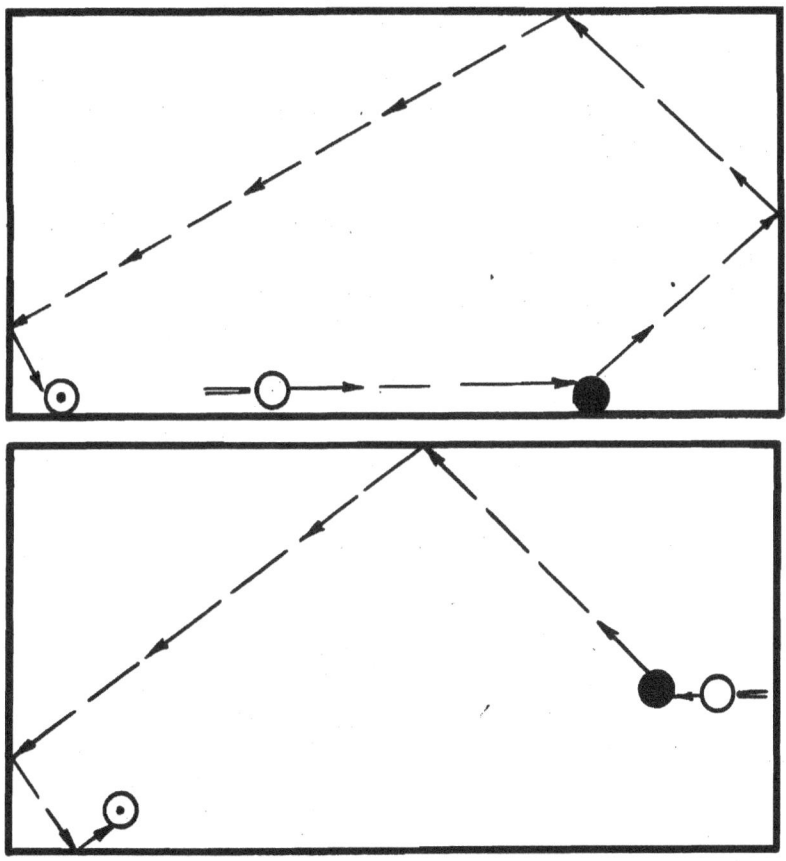

Some typical three-cushion shots: The white cue ball strikes the dark object ball, then caroms off to hit three cushions and the spotted ball.

reasons why I say that balkline is far more difficult.

The physical exertion and mental strain of a championship balkline contest are much greater than in a similar contest at three-cushion. In three-cushion you do not have the draws, close follows, massés, one-cushion shots, and many other technical shots to contend with that are so trying on the nerves.

I am very fond indeed of both games, but I really prefer three-cushion tournament play. It is easier to get in shape and one does not have to go through weeks of hard practice, drilling on technical points of the game and learning to concentrate thoroughly for long periods of time. Three-cushion is a thrilling game to play in competition, matching shot for shot and safety for safety with your opponent. I enjoy this form of competition far more than the more serious and difficult balkline game.

In three-cushion most of the thought and conversation among the players runs to system play, but in the final analysis this resolves itself down to the player's own good judgment and ability to strike the cue ball perfectly at all times. You cannot make three-cushion bank shots by subtracting or adding numbers allotted to various diamonds on the table.

Balkline or straight-rail billiards should be played by people who like to study and have plenty of patience. I can assure you that if you make a serious study of this game for years to come, you will never learn all there is to know about it. No player ever has yet.

Three-cushion billiards is by far the more popular game of the two today, and I believe that it should be. Three-cushion is a great equalizer. If one player outclasses another, it is only necessary to spot probably five in fifty and you have a contest. In balkline if one player is superior to the other, it is almost impossible to arrange a handicap that will make a contest. Besides, the better player will be doing most of the shooting while his opponent is sitting on the sidelines. In the other style of play both players are continually in action, which makes for a close game.

To play three-cushion expertly requires a knowledge of fundamentals equal to that of the balkline player. You require the correct stance, grip, bridge, and stroke—and without them you will be as much of a dub in three-cushion as you would be in balkline. Acquaint yourself with the instructions in the first part of this book, for without them you cannot improve your three-cushion game. This includes the technique of English, draw, and follow shots, for all of these effects are used in the angle game, too.

A good balkline player invariably is a good three-cushion player. The success of balkline experts in three-cushion tournaments is proof of that. The reverse, however, is not always true. Proficiency in the balkline game is a sure step toward expertness in three-cushion. The game you prefer is the one to play. Either will do you much good physically and mentally.

2. The Three-Cushion Shot

EACH three-cushion shot presents an individual problem. It is virtually impossible to set down rules that will cover the selection of every shot you choose to play. There are, however, a few fundamentals which, if followed, will help you make the correct choice and better your chances of scoring.

I continually see players trying to make shots that are impossible—even for the most polished expert. In other words, there just isn't any such shot, but they go blithely along banging the balls around the table and wondering why they can't score. That is why the choice of shots is of such importance in playing three-cushion successfully.

When you are trying to decide which of several shots to play, make your calculations while still standing erect. Usually there are several ways to play the same shot. Avoid the one which involves the possibility of a kiss-off. Avoid shots where excessive power is necessary, for no player can be accurate when using his most powerful stroke. If you watch the great players, you will see that they avoid such shots, all other considerations being equal.

Often you will see that a shot can be attempted off either object ball. In this case, assuming that both methods are equally difficult, play off the ball nearest your cue ball.

To begin with, by playing off the closest object ball, you will be far more accurate. It is logical to assume that you will have more accuracy at a distance of a foot than at eight or ten feet. In addition to accuracy, playing off the closest object ball permits you to put more English on the cue ball. You will find that you have better control of the shot and will be better able to give the cue ball the action you desire.

Shooting at the nearest object ball is not always good policy, of course. Sometimes the easier shot is by playing off the farthest ball first, but unless there is good reason for doing otherwise, take the nearer one.

Another thing to avoid is cuing your ball very high.

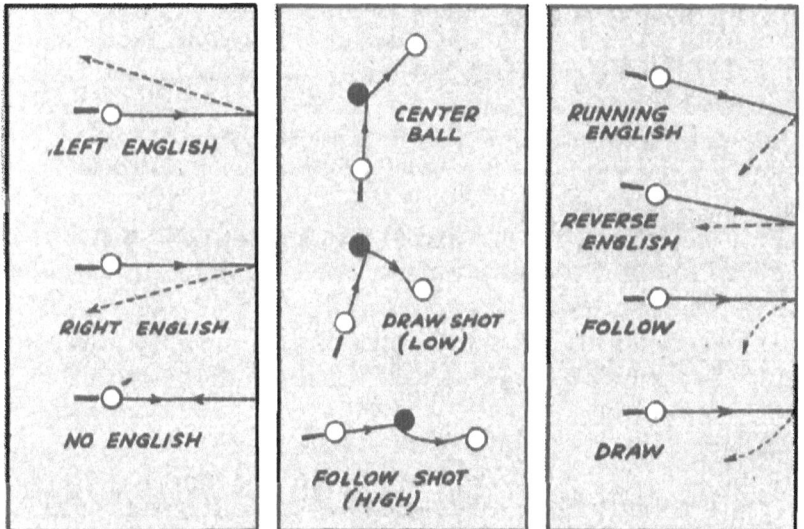

Diagrams showing the effects of English on a cue ball hit to a cushion, and (center) reaction on object ball of cue ball hit in various ways.

LITTLE TECHNICAL LIBRARY

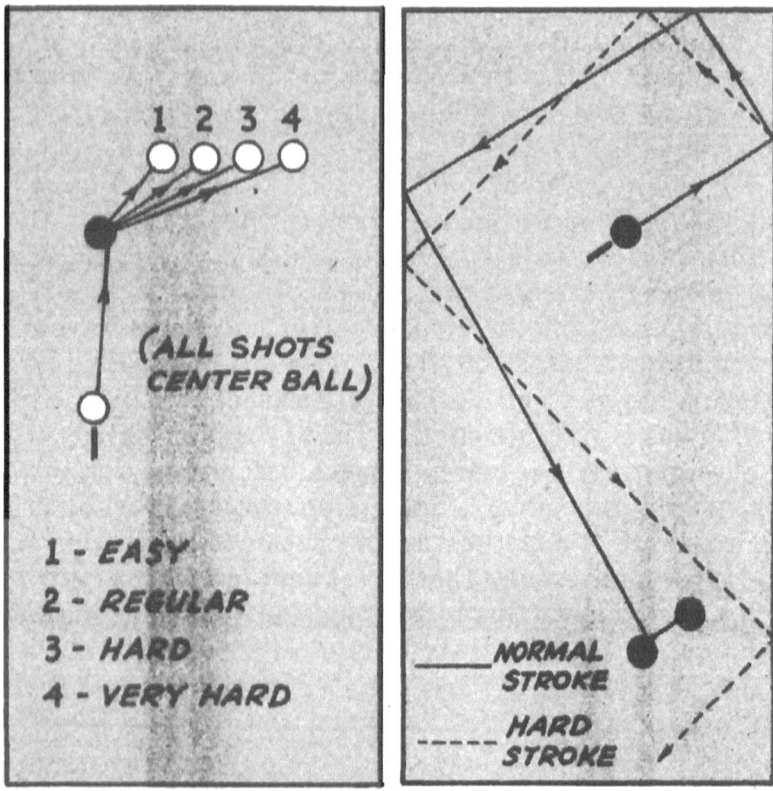

Diagram (left) shows effect of force on a cue ball rebounding off an object ball. Too much force may cause you to miss easy carom (right).

This tends to give it an unnatural action and may cause it to curve after leaving the rail. There are shots where such action is desired, but these are exceptions. In most cases it is best to have the cue ball take a smooth, natural angle in its travel around the table.

The Use of English in Three-Cushions

It is essential in three-cushion to put maximum English on the ball when it is needed. As in balkline, however, the tendency to veer the cue to right or left in an effort to aid the direction of the ball will cause many miscues. Learn to deliver the cue straight through on your line of aim, and you will find that your game will improve vastly.

Do not use English unless you feel it is absolutely necessary in order to get the effect you desire. Remember, too, that when a cue ball strikes the first object ball, the latter will take just the opposite English to that which you put on your cue ball. This will change the direction of the object ball. This principle is used in three-cushion to help avoid kiss-offs. By using excessive English on the cue ball, you change the natural course of the first object ball, thereby allowing the two balls to pass without interference.

In the three-cushion game, where the player must contend with the long and short roll of the table, speed is all-important. The long roll takes place when the cue ball is traveling toward the head of the table, the end which is marked by the manufacturer's nameplate. The short roll is toward the opposite end.

It is absolutely essential to allow for these long and short rolls in three-cushion play. Too much speed on the cue ball will cause the long or short roll to have less effect on the cue ball. Needless to say, if a player does not know how hard the stroke will be, making calculations to allow for these rolls is a hopeless task. The first thing to do is to decide just what power you will use and then base all further calculations on this amount of force.

The effect of varying speed on a shot can be seen with a very simple experiment. Place the object balls on the table so that you can make a three-cushion "natural" bank shot—that is, one in which hitting the cue ball with a natural stroke and no English will make the billiard. Note the action of the ball and the angle it takes as it leaves the cushions. (See diagrams, page 82.)

Now play the same shot, using much more power, and hitting the cue ball in the same spot. You will see a different result. If you select the right spot on the cushion, the first stroke will complete the billiard. On the second you will miss it probably by a foot.

You cannot hope to improve your billiard game by good luck or chance, and if you do not consider at the very start the exact speed you will use, you are simply depending on good fortune rather than skill.

The two most important things necessary to complete a three-cushion shot successfully are: first, perfect speed; and second, hitting the first object ball exactly as you planned.

Your judgment of good speed is based on hitting the object ball in a certain spot. Now assume you make a poor hit and the object ball is struck fuller or thinner than you planned. In the first situation, your cue ball will travel less distance than you planned; and in the second, it will travel farther. In either event, you will find that the speed of your cue ball is far from what you hoped for. This is because your ball has met with either more or less resistance, as the case may be, when coming into contact with the first object ball.

The fuller you strike the object ball, the more force imparted to it and the less speed the cue ball retains. The thinner you strike the first ball, the less force it takes away and the more speed left for the cue ball. The exact spot of contact with the first object ball must be decided upon before you will know just what force to use. These two principles go hand in hand, and both must be considered in all shots.

3. Diamond System

THE "diamond system" is a method of calculating three-cushion angles by means of the diamonds or similar marks spaced around the edges of the billiard table.

There are numerous and varied forms of diamond systems, all more or less mathematically correct. They are based on the theory that a cue ball, hit squarely in the center, will follow a certain path around the table, rebounding from one cushion to hit another at a certain point. Numbers are assigned to the diamonds and angles figured by addition or subtraction.

The diagram on page 86 offers a simple explanation of the system, from which you can probably work out your own theories without delving too deeply into the various texts written on the subject. You will note that the diamonds are numbered. Theoretically, a ball which hits the cushion at No. 1 on the end rail will travel around the table, continuously hitting the other rails at the No. 1 diamonds until it comes to rest. The same holds true for Numbers 2 and 3. Balls which strike Diamonds O and X theoretically will strike the corners marked with similar letters and return.

LITTLE TECHNICAL LIBRARY

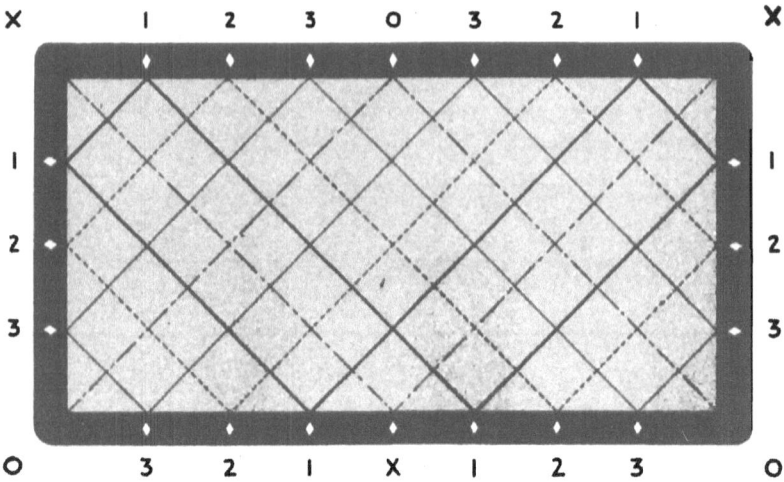

Basis of diamond systems: A ball hitting a cushion at a numbered point and at indicated angle will travel around table hitting all cushions at similarly numbered points. Ball hitting cushion at point X or O will go to corner, then back to cushion, then to other corner similarly marked.

In actual practice, devotees of the diamond system use various methods involving arithmetic, algebra, and even higher mathematics, too involved and, to my mind, too impractical to be worth much space here. But the foregoing is the basis of all these methods, and the theory may be useful in ordinary play if the diagram is memorized.

Diamond systems are not infallible, however, because of many factors. For instance, the speed with which you strike the cue ball has much to do with the angle with which it will leave the cushion. The harder the stroke, the sharper the angle. Also entering into the problem is the matter of how high or how low you strike the ball. A cue ball struck below center has a draw effect off the cushion and takes off the rail at a much sharper angle than if struck at or above center.

Then, too, there are many styles of cushions, some

with sharper angles than others and with varying resiliency. Also, the kind of cloth on the table and the quality of the balls make it necessary to use judgment of your own on the angles, despite the apparent scientific accuracy of the diamond system on paper.

These are some of the reasons why I have never studied or learned the various diamond systems. In the final analysis, you must still consider equipment and follow your own judgment. Occasionally, in world's championship tournaments, I have seen some of our best players miss bank shots by ridiculous margins. Because of the strain of battle they apparently missed a calculation somewhere along the line, but so certain were they of their conclusions that they went right ahead and shot. This wide margin of error could never happen to a player who is in the habit of depending on his own judgment.

Nevertheless, I do not mean to say that the diamond system should not be learned by the average player. It will be a guide for him and no doubt a help to his game, and of course, it will be even more beneficial to a beginner.

All of these systems are based on hitting the cue ball with a smooth, free, follow-through stroke and making the cue ball travel at a normal rate of speed. If you cannot hit in this way, you may as well tear up the system. My advice is to try it, and if it helps you, make use of it. If not, don't be discouraged; for you can become a first-class player without knowing it.

4. Avoiding Kisses

THERE is nothing more exasperating in three-cushion billiards than to see a well-executed shot, on the verge of completion, spoiled by accidental contact with one of the object balls rolling around the table. In billiard parlance, this is a "kiss-off"—and it costs the average player many a point.

No set routine can be mapped out to eliminate kisses in three-cushion play, but certain procedures may be outlined which will help you.

One of the most common causes of kisses is the cue ball's striking the first object ball exactly half full. Both object ball and cue ball will then travel at the same speed in opposite directions, and after striking the various cushions are likely to meet again in the center of the table. I don't mean that you are never to hit the object ball half full, because there are many shots where this must be done. But I mention this to give you some idea of how to make your calculations.

Kisses can sometimes be avoided by adding a little additional speed to the shot; also by striking the cue ball low and getting a draw action off the first cushion.

When playing ordinary "naturals" where the kiss is so common, you should make up your mind in advance whether you will try to make your cue ball go ahead of the object ball or will drive the object ball ahead and make the cue ball come after it. In the first case, it is necessary to strike the first ball thin; in the other, more than half full. If there is doubt in your mind as to whether the kiss can be avoided, go off the other edge of the first object ball to the end rail, instead of to the side rail, as is usually done.

Also remember that there are several ways of making the same shot. Avoid the one where the kiss is likely, even though another choice may be slightly more difficult to execute.

Another thought that is not amiss here is that, all things being equal, it is usually good policy to shoot at the ball nearest you. You will be more accurate in your aim and more effective in your stroke.

Billiard fans marvel at the way experts avoid kiss-offs. You may rest assured that these players make up their minds thoroughly just what they intend to do to avoid the kiss. In this respect they differ greatly from the average player.

If you are constantly getting kissed off on the same type of shots, try striking the object ball fuller, driving it ahead of your cue ball. In the event this fails, try striking the object ball thinner. If both fail, I should certainly look for an entirely different method of playing the shot.

5. Safety Play

NOT so long ago, a player's idea in three-cushion was to prevent his opponent from scoring. The result was that he never took a chance, or "shot out," to use the billiard term. He feared that if he missed, he would leave an opening for his opponent. As a result, this type of player passed up many fine chances to score, thereby cutting down the speed with which he himself scored.

In recent years, however, most players have been converted to the idea of shooting out more frequently. The more often you take a chance, the more often you will score, thus speeding up the game. The first requirement in any sport is to score, and anything that takes away from the ability to do this is poor policy and doomed to failure.

Since Willie Hoppe and other balkline players have taken up three-cushion billiards, the game has speeded up more than in any other period in its history. This is chiefly caused by the fact that the balkline player has considerable knowledge as to where both the object ball and the cue ball will stop, even on hard

SCIENTIFIC BILLIARDS

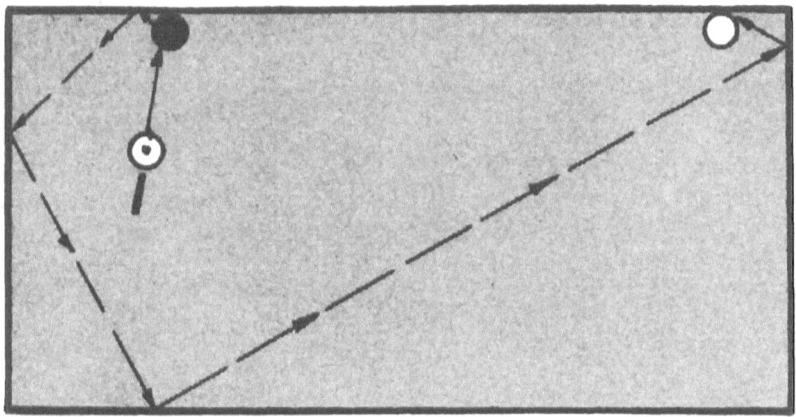

A perfect safety position, if the incoming player has to shoot with the cue ball at right, which is frozen to the cushion. Under the new rules (see note, page 93) safety play has been greatly liberalized.

strokes. With this knowledge he apparently can shoot out on almost every shot and if he misses, still leave the balls in fairly safe position against his opponent.

It is seldom nowadays that you see a player take a deliberate safety, thereby giving up all chance of scoring. There are exceptions, of course, but usually one or

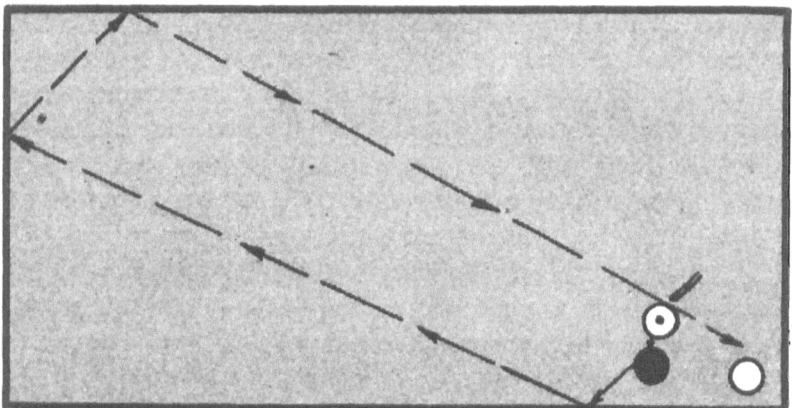

Incoming player forced to shoot with the cue ball at the extreme right faces trouble. Diagram shows ease with which shot could be made if incoming player could use the other ball, as indicated by latest rules.

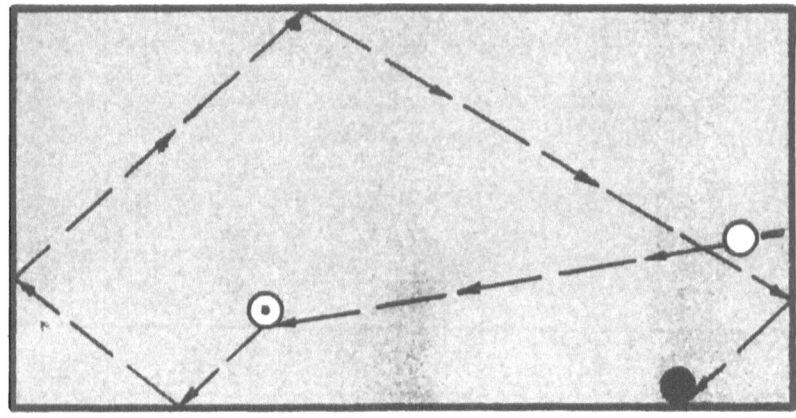

A player required to shoot with the cue ball on the left faces one of the game's most difficult shots—a cross-table attempt with one object ball frozen on cushion. Using other cue ball, shot becomes a natural.

two deliberate safeties in a game will suffice. Years ago ten or even twenty were not unusual.

Like everything else, however, shooting out can be overdone. So can taking chances. A little good judgment when and where to do each is necessary. A player who takes a chance on everything will be no more successful than one who is reluctant ever to risk it.

In three-cushion billiards, knowledge of speed is necessary in safety play. In the old days when the players seldom took a chance, the object was to leave one's own cue ball near the red ball at one end of the table, with the opponent's cue ball at the other end. Today these are considered simple bank shots.

The object of safety play should be to leave your cue ball and the object ball well spread—a foot or more apart—with the opponent's cue ball at the opposite end of the table. Speed of your stroke is the most important factor in such leaves. Striking the ball too gently or too hard will give you an entirely different result from that which you seek.

In playing for a deliberate safety, remember that you must make your cue ball strike the object ball and then a cushion, or force the object ball against a cushion. Failure to do this will result in the loss of a point. Once having played a deliberate safety shot, you must play to score on your next shot or also forfeit a point.*

The best rule is to avoid deliberate safety shots wherever possible. Just try to make your calculations in such a way that, in the event you should miss, the balls will not come to rest in a position which leaves your opponent a natural or comparatively easy shot.

Things to Remember in Three-Cushion

1. Always choose the simplest method of making a shot when more than one way is possible.
2. Make your calculations while standing erect, and avoid shots where too much power is needed.
3. All else being equal, make your shot off the closest object ball.
4. Don't hit your cue ball too high. It will come off the rail at an unnatural angle.
5. Don't use English on three-cushion shots unless it is absolutely essential.
6. The force of your shot must be calculated in advance and not changed, as a difference in speed will make a difference in the angle of the rebound.

---

*Editor's Note—As this book went to press, the Billiard Association of America announced a new rule governing three-cushion play. This rule, designed to speed up tournament play, provides that the first player may select either white ball for a cue-ball. If he counts (scores) with that cue-ball he may again select either ball for his cue-ball, and must then retain that cue-ball for the balance of the half-inning. Thereafter, at the beginning of each half-inning, the incoming player shoots with the still ball (i.e., the white ball not last used as the cue-ball). If he counts, he may choose either white ball for his cue-ball, retaining this ball for the balance of the half-inning.

LITTLE TECHNICAL LIBRARY

SOME THREE-CUSHION SHOTS

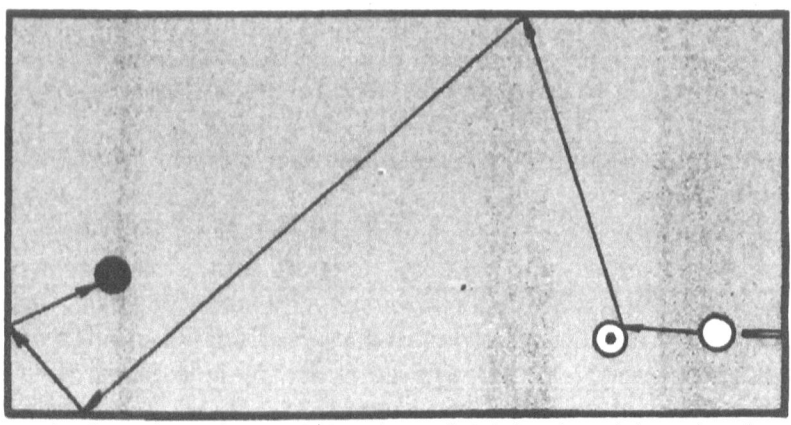

A back-up shot: The cue ball is hit with left-hand English, and with enough force to make it back off third rail into the second object ball.

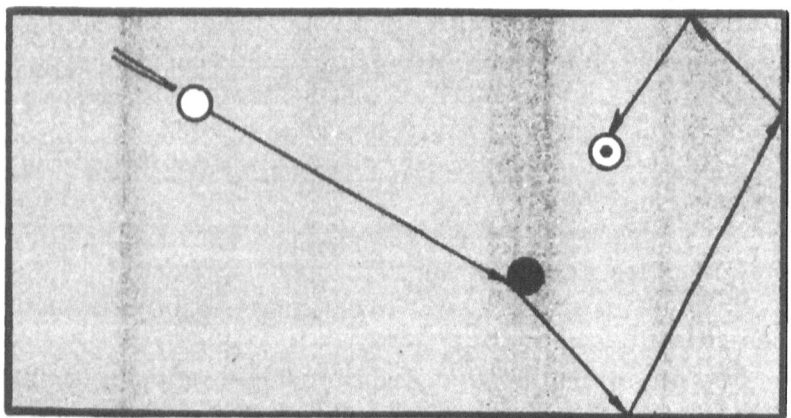

Spin shot: Extreme left English just below center causes cue ball to spin in almost the same spot on contact with first object ball, which can get out of the way of the billiard, without spoiling it by a kiss.

7. Always hit the object ball exactly as you plan—neither fuller nor thinner. Hitting too full will slow up your cue ball; too thin will permit the cue ball to continue at almost the same speed.

8. Learn a diamond system if you want, but it is

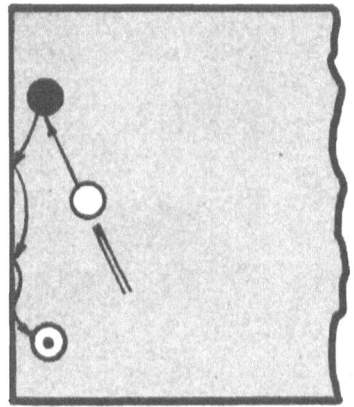 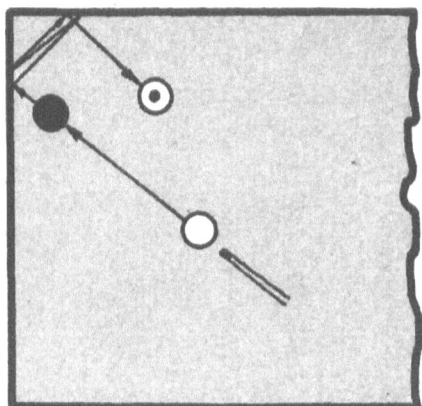

The massé (left): Sharp downward stroke with left English drives cue ball into dark object ball, then back along rail for three bounces before hitting second ball. The four-cushion follow (right) involves right English, hitting through the dark object ball into the left rail. Cue ball bounds back and forth before striking the second ball.

not all-important to three-cushion billiards. Your own good judgment is more vital to success.

9. If a certain type of shot results in kiss-offs, try making the play some other way.

10. Hitting an object ball half full is the most frequent cause of kiss-offs. Remember this in calculating three-cushion shots.

1. Art of Practicing

KNOWING how to practice so as to secure the best results is something in which most billiard players fail miserably. Invariably they will take a set of balls and start playing shot after shot, and, in their own minds, how well they are doing depends upon how many shots they complete successfully. This, to my way of thinking, is anything but true. Instead of considering the scoring angle, they should be practicing and concentrating on the method employed, for whether or not a point is scored means little in practice.

When I started to take lessons, my instructor used only one ball, for the reason that he was teaching me the method of approaching the table and the proper stance. Naturally, these were the things I was to concentrate on. So in your practice, too, why should there be two or three balls on the table to distract you from your principal objective?

A player practicing the draw shot will find he will master the stroke much more quickly if he will eliminate one ball. This will allow him to concentrate fully on driving the object ball, and when he has learned to do this, he will find that he is following through with a smooth, even stroke and that the ball will be coming back in a satisfactory manner. How far it comes back depends upon how low the cue ball is struck and what amount of force is used, something entirely independent of a third ball on the table.

Another shot where two balls should be used during practice is the dead ball, in which the cue ball almost stops after contact with the object ball. If you use three balls, the urge to score the shot will cause you to get too far off center on the first object ball and this will cause the cue ball to travel too fast and too far, taking away the effect you are trying to produce. With only the cue ball and one object ball on the table you are free to concentrate on driving the object ball and striking it near the center, so as to cause your cue ball to move only a short distance.

Another thing which eliminating the third ball will help you to overcome is the faulty delivery of the cue through the ball—in other words, allowing the cue to veer to the left or right when striking through. The player develops this faulty delivery because of his urge to get over to the second object ball and score the billiard, and he allows his cue to go to the left or right according to the position of the second object ball. With this ball eliminated, the player loses the urge, as he has no particular place in mind for his cue ball to travel, and he can devote his entire attention to following through on his line of aim, thereby developing a straight accurate stroke.

After these good points have become fully established and are perfectly natural to you, there will be plenty of time to put all three balls on the table and start learning where and how to hit each shot in order to score the billiard. When you reach this stage, you will find your progress much more rapid.

By taking individual shots with which you have trouble and playing them time after time you will eventually learn the exact way to hit the shot in order to score. Without first acquiring the proper delivery of the cue through the ball, it is impossible to master these shots completely. The time you spend practicing, if done along the lines I have recommended, will allow you to advance much more rapidly and will take you much farther in billiards.

The foundation on which a player's game is based or the method he uses are what govern just how far he may expect to progress in billiards, as in golf, bowling, tennis, or any other sports.

2. In Conclusion

HAVING covered the principal aspects of billiards as played by champions, we have reached an appropriate point for a few general remarks.

Concentrate

Billiards is a game that requires deep concentration to produce the best results. This is one of the many reasons why you should play the game. If you can forget your troubles and business worries while playing billiards, the game will be helpful to you.

Only by entirely concentrating on the shot at hand can you hope to hit the first ball in exactly the right spot or get the correct amount of speed into the shot, avoid the kisses, get the object ball to come back into position, or the like. It takes the greatest of pains and thought to produce these results. Billiard players of the top rank have learned how to concentrate on the play to the exclusion of everything else.

Concentration in balkline play is more difficult because of the long runs, and sometimes it is necessary to maintain this concentration over long periods of time. However, this quality is just as vital in the successful completion of a three-cushion shot. Concentrate on the exact spot of contact on the object ball, exactly where your tip is to hit the cue ball, and the speed you wish to use. If you do this, your chance of success on each shot will increase and your game will improve. You will also find that you have not had time to worry over your outside troubles, and this mental rest should prove beneficial to you.

Be a Good Sport

Billiards should be played for your own pleasure and sport. If you are to derive the greatest benefit from the game, the first requirement is to be a good sport yourself. Players who are forever complaining about the balls rolling off and their bad luck are not as a rule popular with other players. There are also the player who never has a good time unless he is the winner, and the player who always tells his opponent how lucky he was to win. There are many players who blame every miscue on the tip instead of on their faulty stroke, which is usually the real reason.

The players involved in championship play are invariably good sports. They take their defeats well, and they know they must be good losers as well as good winners. When you consider that these men are playing for their livelihood, it is not too much to expect amateurs to show the same fine spirit. Of course most players do, but in every group there are a few who must have an "alibi" for each missed shot or lost game. Needless to say, these players are not popular. To one of this type I suggest that he quit blaming the equipment, his own bad luck, and his opponent's good fortune for his downfall, and look for his own faults. They are the real cause of his failure.

Just remember that you should be playing billiards for the pleasure you get out of the game. Your opponent plays for the same reason, and if he has to listen to your complaints about equipment, about his great good luck, and your own exceptionally bad luck, he will have a hard time enjoying the game. Eliminate these complaints; you will enjoy the game more yourself, and your opponent certainly will. You will also soon find yourself much more popular.

Learn to Criticize Your Shots

Learn to criticize your own mistakes intelligently. Missing shots without figuring out exactly why you did not get the correct result is a double waste.

For years my teacher made me give him the exact cause of every miss during the lesson period. This is not easy to do without study and knowledge of the action of billiard balls. There are many different factors involved, one depending on another, and any one of several mistakes may cause the shot to be a failure.

Figuring out just what the error was before going to the next shot, will, over a period of time, vastly improve your game. If you can solve successfully the cause of the missed shot, it will naturally be far easier to correct the mistake on the next practice stroke. Too many people just "skip it" and try the shot again.

You should be able to tell why you failed if you will consider the path the first object ball takes, the angle the cue ball takes when leaving the object ball, and also the position of all three balls when the shot is completed.

If you can decide that the object ball was struck

too thin or too full, or the cue ball too high or too low, or that improper speed was used, or pick out any other cause for failure, it is a simple matter to make changes and in time learn exactly how to hit the shot for the best results.

A player who simply keeps practicing the same shot over and over without being able to tell why the shot went astray may find himself failing indefinitely. Only by analyzing why you went wrong and then correcting the fault can you get the most out of your practice and your playing.

Conclusion

If you do not get good results in a day or a week, do not become discouraged. Remember, it is not more knowledge of shots that you need to improve your game, but more accurate and effective delivery of your cue. Greater and faster improvement will come in your game from improving your form.

Try not to be impatient with yourself. It is not easy to change your stance, your method of holding or swinging the cue, or any of the other phases of the game in which you have been violating good form. It takes long, hard practice to overcome some faults.

Check through the pages of this book, see wherein your faulty play lies, and then follow the suggested method of practice to get the best results.

You'll find that you'll soon be playing better and better billiards—and deriving greater pleasure from a game which boasts every essential for both recreation and enjoyment.

Good luck to all of you—and may your points come in clusters!

BILLIARD TALK

balls—2⅜ inches in diameter, made of ivory or composition, two being white and used as cue balls. One of these has a distinguishing black dot. The third is red and is always an object ball. In pocket games there are sixteen balls, 2¼ inches in diameter. One white ball is used as a common cue ball by both or all players, the rest are colored or banded in a distinguishing manner and are numbered from one to fifteen.

balklines. Lines drawn on the table eighteen inches from each rail and parallel to the rails, forming eight spaces around the edge of the playing surface. These spaces are known as balk spaces. Additional balk spaces seven inches square, placed at all points where the balklines meet the rails are called anchor blocks.

banking. Method used to determine which player has the choice of starting or declining to start a game. Consists of driving the cue ball from head end of table to the opposite end rail and back. Shot returning closest to head rail gives that player the choice. Also called lagging or stringing.

bank shot. A shot in which one or more cushions are struck by the cue ball before it strikes the first object ball.

balance. Term usually used in reference to cues, the balance point of most cues being about where the wrapping ends closest to the tip, usually fourteen to seventeen inches from the butt end.

billiard. A point made by striking the two object balls according to the type of game being played. (Also called **carom.**)

body English. Act of trying, by body motions, to make the ball go to the proper place after it has been struck. A complete waste of effort, and in a class with wishful thinking.

bridge. The method of placing the hand and fingers to provide a firm foundation for the tip end of the cue in making a shot. Also a device used to permit players to reach a cue ball at the far end of the table. ——**long bridge.** A bridge in which more than the average six or eight inches of cue travel beyond the fingers in making the stroke.——**short bridge.** A bridge in which only two or three inches of cue project beyond the bridge. (A long bridge is used for driving the ball; a short one for delicate shots.)

butt. The handle or large end of the cue.

carom. See **billiard.**

count (*v*). To score.

cue. The tapered maple stick with which the player shoots. It is fitted with a leather tip.

crotch. The stroke in which a player hits the ball and cushion at the same time when a ball is touching a cushion. Also a crotch shot.

cue ball. The ball with which the player shoots.

cushion. Triangular-shaped strips of rubber with which the inner sides of the table are lined. (Also called **rails.**)

cushion carom. A point made by striking the two object balls, during which the cue ball strikes at least one cushion before completing the carom.

dead ball. Method of striking an object ball full so that the cue ball will come almost to a stop.

diamond system. Mathematical process of calculating angles in three-cushion billiards by the use of the diamond along the rails.

draw. Method of striking the cue ball low so that it will tend to return in the direction of the shot after hitting an object ball.

draw back. That portion of the strike in which the cue is drawn away from the cue ball.

English. Method of striking a cue ball to the right or left which imparts spin and changes its direction after hitting an object ball or cushion.

follow. Method of striking a cue ball high so that it will have a tendency to continue in almost a straight line after striking an object ball.

follow-through. The act of continuing the cue in the same direction without pausing after hitting the cue ball.

foot of table. The end of the table not marked by the manufacturer's name plate.

force. Speed with which the cue ball is struck.

foul. An unfair shot, such as hitting the ball twice on the same stroke, jumping the ball off the table, touching the ball with anything other than the cue tip, or shooting the wrong cue ball. The player loses his inning.

frozen ball. A ball which is resting against either another ball or a cushion.

full hit. Striking the object ball at its center with the cue ball.

grip. The manner in which the butt of the cue is held before and during a shot.

half-full shot. Striking the object ball either to the right or left of center with the cue ball.

head of table. The end of the table marked by the manufacturer's name plate. All games start at the head end of the table.

SCIENTIFIC BILLIARDS

inning. A player's turn to shoot. He continues until he misses, fouls or concludes the game.

in hand. A ball is in hand after jumping the table or if, when the balls are frozen, the player elects to have them spotted.

kiss or kiss-off. Accidental contact by the cue ball or one of the object balls with another ball. Usually this spoils the shot, although there are occasions when a kiss will complete a carom which otherwise would be missed.

lagging. Determining who shall start a game by each contestant's shooting a ball to the opposite end of the table and back. The one whose ball stops nearest the starting end of the table has the choice of shooting first or making his opponent take the lead. Also called **banking** or **stringing**.

massé. A shot in which the cue ball is struck with the cue held almost perpendicular to the table.

miscue. A stroke in which the cue slips off the cue ball, spoiling the shot.

natural. A term used to describe a shot in which the object balls are in such position that it is almost impossible to miss the point if the first object ball is hit correctly.

nip draw. A draw shot where the cue ball and first object ball are very close together. When the balls are less than one inch apart the play would be considered a nip draw.

nurse. Method of controlling the balls in billiards so that long runs are possible.

object ball. The ball at which a player shoots.

pockets. The receptacles at the four corners and at the middle of the long sides of the billiard table into which the players attempt to shoot the balls in playing pocket billiards.

pool. Another name for pocket billiard games, which, owing to low associations, is no longer in popular favor.

push shot. Pushing cue ball instead of striking it. Also striking the cue ball twice on the same stroke. (Both fouls.)

rail. See **cushion.**

rack. Triangular-shaped frame used to place the balls properly on the table in pocket billiard games.

rail nurse. A nurse in which the balls are kept in position along the rails. One object ball is kept very near the rail, the other out from the rail about three inches and slightly ahead of the inside ball. The outside ball is moved continually on a line parallel to the rail while the inside ball is driven lightly against the rail and out again slightly.

reverse English. English placed on the side of the ball opposite to the side on which the object ball is to be hit.

run. The number of billiards a player makes in any one inning. In pocket billiards, the number of balls driven into the pockets in any one inning.

running English. English placed on the side of the ball on which the object ball is to be hit, or in the direction of the angle at which the cue ball is to rebound from the cushion.

safety. In three-cushion billiards, a shot in which no effort is made to score, the player attempting instead to ensure a difficult shot for the opponent.

scratch. A shot in which the cue ball fails to hit either object ball. This is usually penalized by the loss of a point. In pocket billiards, when the cue ball goes into a pocket.

shooting out. A three-cushion term indicating that a player is trying for points, regardless of safety play.

spot. A point halfway across a line drawn from the second diamond on one long side of the table to the second diamond on the other long side.

spot *(v.).* To place a ball on the spot mark.

spread draw. Draw shot where the cue ball travels some distance to the right or left of the first object ball before completing the carom.

stance. The position of the feet and body prior to and during a shot.

striker. The player who is having his inning at the table.

string. The line drawn between the second diamonds at the head end of the table.

stringing. See **banking**.

stroke. The act of shooting the cue ball.

thin hit. Striking the object ball with the cue ball almost at its very edge.

three-cushion carom. A billiard or point made by striking the two object balls with the cue ball, which has struck three or more cushions before completing the carom.

www.ingramcontent.com/pod-product-compliance
Lightning Source LLC
Chambersburg PA
CBHW021812220426
43662CB00006B/285